Presentations
Plus

Second Edition

Presenting, Persuading, and Winning

Although I've been in the computer business most of my life, we're not here to talk about:

- HARDWARE
- SOFTWARE
- OR APPLICATIONS

(Notice the list of three)

What we're here to talk about is:

- MONEY
- FAME
- AND GLORY

(Another list of three — more about threes in Chapter 6)

More specifically, we're going to talk about how to get more business with less effort by doing the right things the first time. And if you're not interested in that, we will also talk about how you can become too valuable to keep in your present job *at your present pay*.

Now, I have a question for the ladies. You guys tune me out. The question is this. How many frogs do you have to kiss to find a prince? The answer is—lots. Or in the terminology of the business we're in, how many clients, customers, or prospects do we have to chase to get one order? The answer is—*lots*. My experience is that I have to chase four to catch one, or a marketing effectiveness of 25%. What if for every four we chased, we could catch not one but two—or a marketing effectiveness of 50%. This would mean a *100% increase* in our marketing effectiveness!

Let's talk about our job. I would like to suggest to you that whatever we do, wherever we work, a key part of our job is to persuade other people to a course of action we would like them to take.

If you buy that, then I would like to recommend that when your time comes to persuade others, you stand up and give a presentation using visual aids—as opposed to just talking across a desk. I say that because a

Presentations Plus

Second Edition

David Peoples' Proven Techniques

David A. Peoples
Atlanta, Georgia

John Wiley & Sons

New York • Chichester • Brisbane • Toronto • Singapore

Library of Congress Catalog in Publication Data
Peoples, David A., 1930-
   Presentations plus : David Peoples' proven techniques / by David
   A. Peoples. — 2nd ed.
      p. cm.
      ISBN 0-471-55926-1. — ISBN 0-471-55956-3 (pbk.)

   1. Business presentations   I. Title.
HF5718.22.P44   1992
658.4'5—dc20   92-57
                                                                CIP
Printed in the United States of America
10   9   8   7   6
Printed and bound by Courier Companies, Inc.

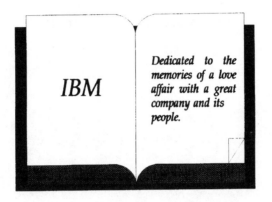

IBM

Dedicated to the memories of a love affair with a great company and its people.

PREFACE

Make thyself a craftsman in speech, for thereby thou shalt gain the upper hand.

Inscription found in a
3,000-year-old Egyptian tomb

How proud I am that the first edition of this book won the Maeventec Award for excellence in style, content, and format.

This second edition contains major enhancements and updated material. New chapters are:

Chapter 1—Presenting, Persuading, and Winning
(Money, fame, and glory)

Chapter 7—High Tech vs. Low Tech
(When to use *what* to accomplish the most)

Chapter 12—DOs and DON'Ts of Team Presentations
(The very few vs. the thundering heard)

Chapter 16—Presentation Planning Guide
(Guarantees a winning presentation every time)

This is a book on how to develop and deliver an effective and exciting presentation.

It comes from success on the battlefield of business. It is based on years of doing, not on theory. Its methods are simple, practical, and proven. Its approach is effective when presenting to clients, customers, and prospects. It works equally well when used by managers or trainees.

The techniques of *Presentations Plus* have proven successful in the executive suite, the conference room, and the classroom. They are equally effective with an audience of one or an audience of hundreds.

The overall thrust of this book is to help you achieve your objectives and get results.

If you are presenting to clients, customers, or prospects, this book will show you how to get more business with less effort by doing the right things the first time.

If you are presenting within your organization, this book will show you how to become too valuable to keep in your present job at your present pay.

If you want results, this book will show you how to persuade other people to a course of action you would like them to take.

If time is short and the pressure is great, and you could use some quick help, we have some quick answers. Read "The Seven Deadly Sins" (Chapter 2), then turn to "The Presentation Planning Guide" (Chapter 16) and follow the instructions. Next, fine-tune your presentations with "60 Tips in 60 Minutes" (Chapter 15). Finally, if your heart beats fast and your nerves are tight and your palms are a little sweaty, you might want to check out "Hot Drugs for Sweaty Palms" (Chapter 3).

In every company and organization there is a critical shortage of good presenters. If you learn to do well what most do so poorly, your success will be faster and further.

So come along with me. Let's walk this road together. And, I believe, you will walk the road to glory.

David A. Peoples
Author and Speaker

Atlanta, Georgia
November, 1991

Note: Anyone wishing to correspond with the author may do so at P.O. Box 8850, Longboat Key, FL 34228.

A C K N O W L E D G E M E N T S

CLIP ART COURTESY OF

3M Company
Heading for Chapters 2,6,9,11

Artmaster Book Company
Heading for Chapters 10,14,16,17

Graphic Products Corp.
Heading for Chapter 13

Dover Publications
Heading for Chapter 15

CONTENTS

C O N T E N T S

Presentations Plus

*If all my talents were to be taken from me
by some unscrutable Providence, and I
had my choice of keeping but one, I would
unhesitatingly ask to be allowed to keep
the Power of Speaking, for through it I
would quickly recover all the rest.*

— Daniel Webster

study done at the University of Minnesota revealed that if you stand up and give a presentation using visual aids, your audience, your client, or your prospect is *43% more likely to be persuaded.*

FIGURE 1A Results of Presenting vs. Talking.

A bombshell came out of that study—unexpected, unanticipated by anybody: If you stand up and give a presentation, your customer, client, or prospect will be willing to pay *26% more money* for the same product or service.

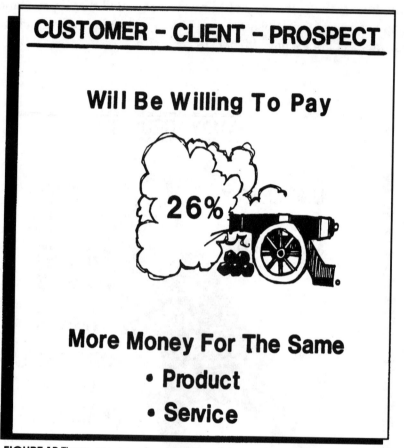

FIGURE 1B There are good reasons for giving a stand-up presentation.

There's more smoking gun evidence. Let's go to the Wharton School of Business at the University of Pennsylvania for a look at a controlled study of a presentation to try to persuade people to invest their money in a new business.

In that study, Group A told their story sitting down talking across the table. When it was over, 58% said, "I will sign up for that business proposition." Group B used the same facts, same numbers, same statistics. Everything was identical with two exceptions: first, the presenter stood up, and second, the presenter used visuals aids. Now, not 58% but 79% said, "I will sign up for that business proposition."

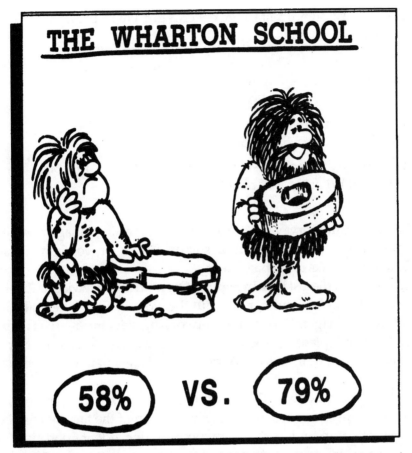

FIGURE 1C Results of sitting down and talking vs. standing up and presenting.

Moreover, the presenter who stood up and used visual aids was perceived by the audience as being:

- More professional
- More persuasive
- More credible
- More interesting
- And better prepared

There are also significant fringe benefits to giving a presentation using visual aids.

Learning is improved up to 200%.
  Study at University of Wisconsin

Retention is improved up to 38%.
  Studies at Harvard and Columbia

Time to explain complex subjects is reduced by 25% to 40%.
  Study at Wharton School of Business

Did you see the survey in *USA Today* on women in management? The survey ranked and rated the critical success factors for women who have made it to the ranks of management.

Take a look at the last item in Figure 1D. The item ranked last is the item some people think is number one. But the women who have made it to the ranks of management say the "networking" factor ranks last in their book. In second place is problem solving and decision making. But the number one critical success Factor ranked by the women who have made it big is *communication skills.*

And did you hear about the survey of faculty members of engineering schools? The results were startling. The opinion of the faculty members was that 15% of an engineer's future success is dependent upon his or her engineering skills, while *85%* depends upon their *communication skills.*

The critical message is this: In the minds of your audience, your client, your customer, or your prospect, the quality of your presentation is a mirror image of the quality of:

- Your product
- Your service
- Your support
- And your people

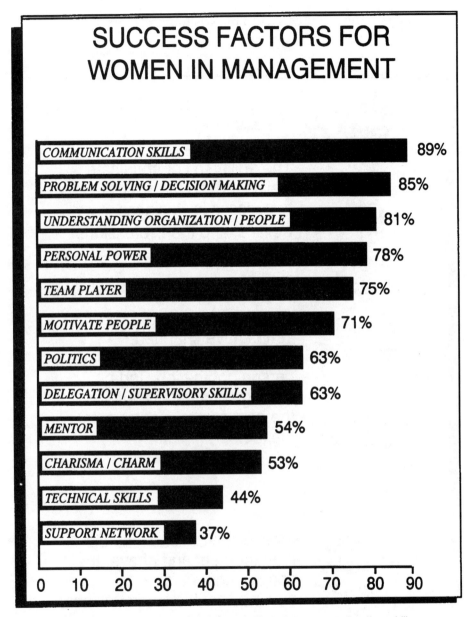

FIGURE 1D The queen of the mountain is communication skills.

So listen up folks and check out the wisdom in Figure 1E.

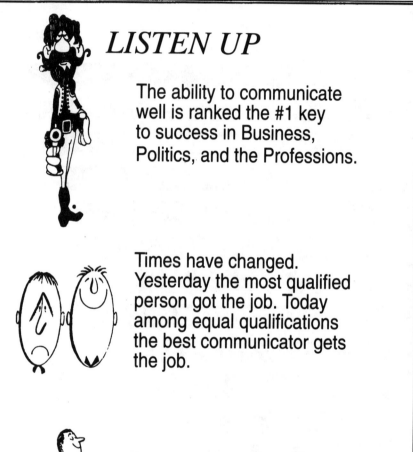

LISTEN UP

The ability to communicate well is ranked the #1 key to success in Business, Politics, and the Professions.

Times have changed. Yesterday the most qualified person got the job. Today among equal qualifications the best communicator gets the job.

As executives reach middle management and above, the primary criteria for advancement is communication and motivation skills rather than basic job performance.

FIGURE 1E

Proof of the above comes from a survey conducted by one of the top ten executive search firms in the country. It was a survey of executives making over $250,000 a year. The survey asked those executives to rank the factors to which they attributed their having made it to the big time. Not surprisingly, the number one factor in their opinion was communication skills.

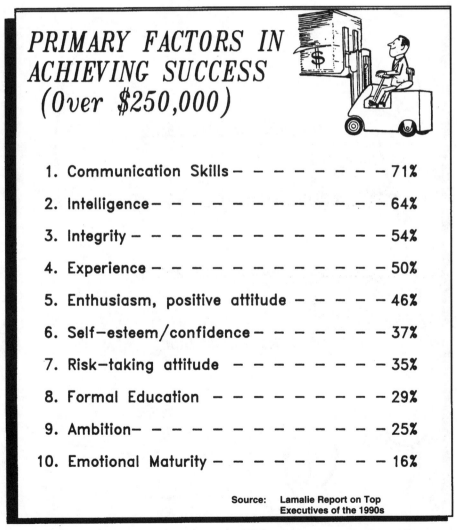

PRIMARY FACTORS IN
ACHIEVING SUCCESS
(Over $250,000)

1. Communication Skills – – – – – – – – 71%

2. Intelligence – – – – – – – – – – – – 64%

3. Integrity – – – – – – – – – – – – – 54%

4. Experience – – – – – – – – – – – – 50%

5. Enthusiasm, positive attitude – – – – – 46%

6. Self–esteem/confidence – – – – – – – 37%

7. Risk–taking attitude – – – – – – – – 35%

8. Formal Education – – – – – – – – – 29%

9. Ambition – – – – – – – – – – – – – 25%

10. Emotional Maturity – – – – – – – – – 16%

Source: Lamalie Report on Top
           Executives of the 1990s

FIGURE 1F The road to the big time starts with communication skills.

People spend years in school and in training, learning and fine-tuning the skills of their profession. Yet they spend almost no time learning the skills to communicate. They do not realize that brilliance without the ability to communicate is worth as little today as it was in the days of Pericles. (Figure 1G).

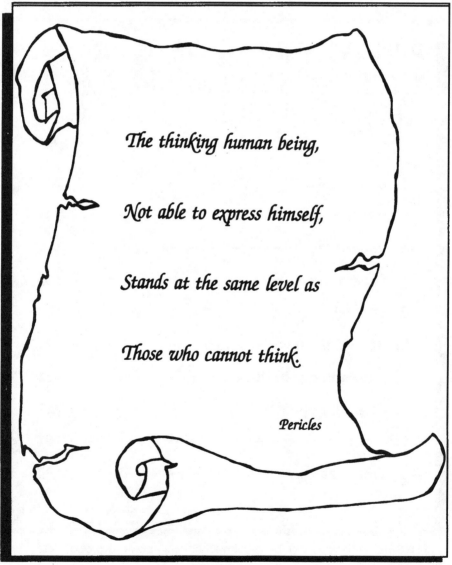

FIGURE 1G

It is a rare situation where one can have a successful and rewarding career communicating only with computers or test tubes. As your world becomes more complex, the ability to communicate those complexities in concise terms becomes more important and more critical to your career. Presentations come with the territory.

Research by the American Society for Training and Development concluded that "the only thing that ranks above communication skills as a factor in work place success is job knowledge."

Yet there is a critical shortage of good presenters. How many good presenters do you think there would be in the typical IBM marketing branch office? The most common answer is somewhere between zero and none. The reason? The good ones have all been promoted!

So if you're looking for a horse to ride to get ahead, just become a good presenter. Notice I didn't say "excellent"—I didn't say "outstanding." Just become *good*—because the rest of the world is so terrible. You will do well if you just do "good" what most do so poorly. And you will become too valuable to keep in your present job at your present pay. If you're not interested for yourself, think of your children—don't they deserve wealthy parents?

Please do not accept the myth that good speakers and presenters are born, not made. Lies—all lies. Speaking and presenting are skills that we learn through desire, effort, and practice. As with any other learned skill, some are better at it than others. But wherever you are on the scale today, I promise you that you can be three times better tomorrow.

Is it worth the effort? You bet your sweet apples it is. Good communication skills can change the lives of people, and alter the course of history.

Let me tell you the stories of three people.

A man started writing a book while in prison for conspiracy against the local people. That book contained the following quote, "All great, world-shaking events have been brought about, not by written matter but by the spoken word."

Our second man was the mortal enemy of the first. He honed his communication skills while a member of parliament. He would later need those skills to rally a people and save a nation.

The third man suffered from a crippling disability, yet he led us out of our greatest financial crisis, and defeated the first man in our greatest encounter.

The book the first man wrote was *Mein Kampf*. Before he took his own life, Adolph Hitler had inflamed a nation with his oratory—and killed thirty million people.

Hitler's mortal enemy was short, fat, and hunchbacked. Yet the ringing words of Winston Churchill brought England from its darkest days to its finest hour.

The third man was our president who was elected most often and served the longest. It is no accident that Franklin Roosevelt was our greatest communicator.

You may not aspire to be a player on the stage of history. Yet in your own world your life can be different and better, and your future brighter. So why not be what you can become?

People say to me, "Well, when the day comes that I have to stand up in front of 20, 50, or a few hundred people, I will prepare a presentation and make some visual aids. But most of my activity in persuading other people is one on one."

May I communicate to you the single most effective technique I have ever found for winning? It is a one-on-one stand-up presentation, with a single person alone with me in a conference room. I know it sounds silly to give a stand-up presentation to one person, but the psychology and the impact is overpowering. Here's why.

YOU WILL BE A BREED APART

Most people have never in their lives had anyone give them a one-on-one stand up presentation. The signal that you send, and the unspoken message, says to him or her, "I'm putting you on a pedestal. I'm making you king or queen for a day. This decision and your business is so important to me and my company that I've organized and formalized my story. You deserve the best I've got to give. I believe that my product or service is so good, and so aligned with your goals and your objectives, that if I can only do my job well of communicating your importance and my conviction well, then I believe we will walk the road together."

The power of this unspoken message as demonstrated by your actions is overwhelming. The enemy will not have a chance. He or she will do what everybody else does, that is, follow the course of least resistance and talk across the desk. What a study in contrast. You will have differentiated yourself from your competitor in a dramatic way. In the words of the stockbroker, you will be a "breed apart."

MORE BUSINESS—LESS EFFORT—LESS TIME

The results of a study published in the *Harvard Business Review* showed that there are an average of seven decision makers in a capital goods decision, and five decision makers in a services/supplier decision. That means if we are doing our job, we will need to call on five to seven people, and tell our story five to seven times.

That's going to take a lot of time. Now the only thing we all have the same amount of is time—but one of the biggest differences between us is how we use it.

Suppose, for example, I call on the key decision maker and say, "Mr. or Ms. Decision Maker, I would like to have the opportunity to give a formal presentation on my products or services to you and the other people involved in this decision." What I am doing is using a formal presentation as the catalyst to get all the decision makers together so that I can present my story one time professionally, instead of seven times unprofessionally.

IT AIN'T OVER UNTIL . . . ALL QUESTIONS ARE ANSWERED

In addition to differentiating yourself from your competitor and saving a lot of time, you will most likely also find that the synergism of the group will tend to get all the pertinent questions on the table. All in attendance will hear the answers to the others' questions. So when it's over, it's more likely to be over and not require follow-up marketing with answers to isolated questions.

CHARGE A HIGHER PRICE

The professionalism you exhibit by giving a presentation will tend to eliminate (or at least minimize) requests for concessions or special contractual arrangements. Even if concession requests are not eliminated, you are more likely to get acceptance of your standard price and contract if you stick to them with a professional image, than you are if you convey the image of a wheeler-dealer talking across the table, peddling a commodity, with the focus on price and delivery.

THE VERY FEW WHO ARE OUTSTANDING

How many teachers have you had in your entire life? Let's include presenters. How many people have stood up in front of you? Let's go back to kindergarten, grade school, college, Sunday school, Boy Scout meetings, Girl Scout meetings—would you agree that it's been hundreds? Let's say 300 to 400. If you've had 300 to 400 people stand up in front of you in your entire life, then let me ask you this question. Of those people, how many were truly outstanding? I've asked that question around the world, and whatever the land and whatever the language, the answer is almost always the same. Most people say three, four, five, maybe six. Most people say, "I could count them on my fingers and have fingers left over."

Next question. Here's the president of a company. He's been president for 20 years. In 20 years, how many marketing/salespeople have called on him—bankers, stockbrokers, insurance salespeople, computer salespeople? Let's say the answer is 300 to 400. If you turned to that president and said, "Mr./Ms. President, of the 300 to 400 salespeople you've seen in the last 20 years, how many were truly outstanding?" What do you think he would say? I think he would say, "I could count them on my fingers and have fingers left over."

Well, what is it about those very few that makes them outstanding? We can get some insight into that from a survey of 12,000 students about their teachers. The question was asked, "What are the characteristics of the very few teachers who were outstanding?" Take a look at their answers in Figure 1H.

Now I ask you, of these characteristics, how many have to do with knowledge of the subject? The answer is one. Only one has to do with knowledge of the subject. Yet where do we spend all our time? On that one! There are eleven other things that are important to your audience.

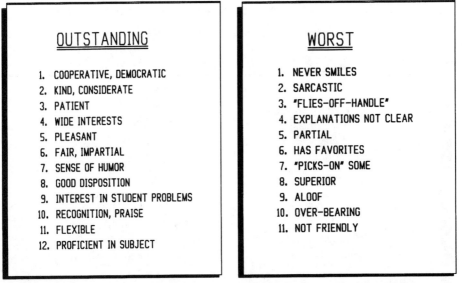

FIGURE 1H Characteristics of the best.   FIGURE 1I Characteristics of the worst.

That was the good news. The bad news is in Figure 1I. Again I say to you, of those characteristics, how many have to do with explaining the subject itself? And again, the answer is one.

So it is that our audience, our clients and our prospects are sending to you and to me a simple message that we do not hear in the complexity of the subject we're presenting. And the simple message that we do not hear is one that says: **Before I Care How Much You Know, I Want to Know How Much You Care.**

This message was understood 2,400 years ago by Aristotle. In his book *Rhetoric*, Aristotle describes what is required to persuade another person to a course of action we would like them to take. He said three things are necessary.

First, we must appeal to the LOGOS (logic).

But, said Aristotle, logic is not enough. We must also appeal to the PATHOS (emotions).

Other observers of human nature have come to the same conclusion. Dale Carnegie said, "When dealing with people, remember you are not dealing with creatures of logic but with creatures of emotion."

And J. P. Morgan said, "A person usually has two reasons for doing something. One that sounds good, and a real reason."

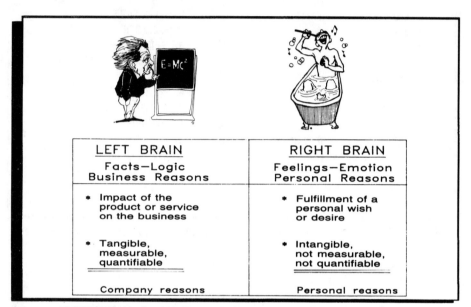

FIGURE 1J We tend to have two reasons for doing something.

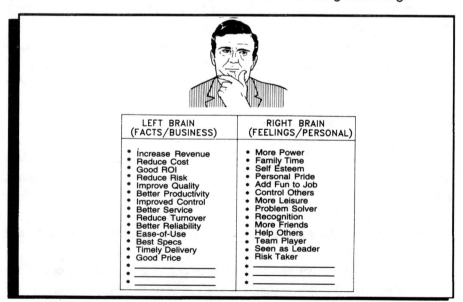

FIGURE 1K To persuade we should appeal to both sides of the brain.

Aristotle said the third requirement is ETHOS—a Greek word which means "disposition, character," and says people tend to do business with people they like, trust, and have confidence in.

And so we conclude this chapter on presenting, persuading, and winning by observing that the natural tendency of human beings is to:

JUSTIFY ON FACTS, BUT BUY ON FEELING.

JUSTIFY WITH BUSINESS REASONS, BUT BUY FOR PERSONAL REASONS.

JUSTIFY WITH LOGIC, BUT BUY ON EMOTION.

My own experience over all these years has led me to the simple conclusion of Figure 1M.

FIGURE 1L The decision process.   **FIGURE 1M** The final answer.

The very best and most effective way to present the facts, appeal to the emotions, and instill trust and confidence is to give a presentation. If you do, your client or prospect is more likely to want to do business with you. The way to win is to understand what the enemy is doing—

and don't do it. Do something different and better. We must differentiate ourselves from our competitors. The competitor is talking across the desk—don't do it. Stand up and give a presentation using visual aids. You will win.

But look out for the Seven Deadly Sins.

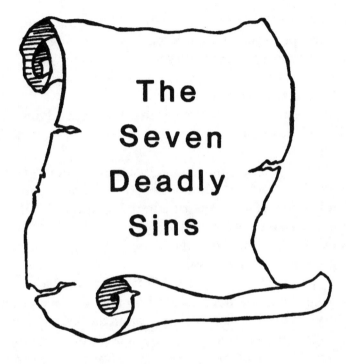

The
Seven
Deadly
Sins

Here are seven guaranteed ways to give a dull, dry, and boring presentation. I learned them from IBM executives.

SIN #1   Show an Organization Chart, Tell the History of Your Department, and Apologize in Advance.

It happens all the time. Here come the hot-shots flying in from the home office to make a presentation to the locals. Through some misguided sense of direction they feel compelled to show you, as the very first thing, an organizational chart of their department and where it fits into the grand scheme of things back at Headquarters.

Then their keen sensitivity tells them that you are just dying to know the details of the history of their department back through the last three reorganizations.

Finally, just so you will understand that they're not incompetent (just busy), they will apologize for the out-of-date material, the small print that you can't read, the spelling errors, running over time, and the fact that they have to leave to catch a plane.

The irony of all this is that they think they're giving a good presentation and telling you just what you want to know.

In fact, the people most interested in an organization chart are the people who are on the organization chart. And the only people who are interested in the history of a department are the people in the department—and half of them aren't interested. As for all the apologizing, I sometimes would like to say to them, "Instead of apologizing for the way it is, explain to me why you haven't corrected it." I betcha that would get it fixed real quick!

SIN #2   Do Not Explain Any Reason Why the Subject Has Any Value to the Audience.

If you cannot articulate a reason for the audience to pay attention to what you have to say, then you have nothing to say to the audience. And that's the problem. Many presentations are put together for a mass audience, with no tailoring and no spice, to present material that's of great interest to the presenter, but of little interest to the audience.

Here's the acid test. How many people do you think would show up if you charged them ten bucks a head to get in to hear what you have to say?

SIN #3   Use a Presentation Designed for One Audience—for a Different Audience.

This is my all-time favorite sin. You can spot this sin in the first 60 seconds. These presenters usually start their presentations with—guess what?—an organization chart. Their purpose was to update Headquarters' management on the wonderful job their department is doing. That same presentation is then delivered to the troops in the field. Do you think they care?

Another example is the use of an internal presentation of a new product as a sales presentation to prospects. Do you think the position of a product within a product line has anything to do with why a prospect should buy it?

SIN #4   Tell the Audience More Than They Want to Know.

This sin is worse than just boring an audience—it is self-defeating. I would guess that over 90% of all presentations could be given in less time and more effectively. And often in *substantially* less time.

Let's look at it this way. You have heard hundreds of presentations. Have you ever sat through a presentation and at the end of it heard anyone say, "It was a great presentation, but it was too short." No. People are more likely to say that it was terrible and too long. After all, the Biblical story of creation is only 600 words long. An if CBS can tell us the world news in just 30 minutes, maybe we can tell our story in less time than we think. Voltaire said, "The secret of being a bore is to tell everything."

A presentation is like a wheel. The longer the spoke, the bigger the tire.

SIN #5   Turn the Lights Out and Show Slides or Transparencies While Reading a Script.

How many presentations like this have you had to sit through? And what if it's right after lunch? And what about that script? Do you think the person reading it is the person who wrote it? (Or was it an English major from Berkeley?) And don't you feel sorry for them when they get out of sync and the words are one step ahead or behind the slides? And what about the close? When the lights come on, the audience en masse will blink their eyes, shake their heads, yawn, and stretch. What drama.

SIN #6   Read Verbatim Every Word on Every Visual.

If your entire presentation consists of nothing but reading verbatim every word on every visual, then the audience can with good reason say, "I don't have to come to your meeting. Just mail me a copy of the handout. I can read." 'Nuff said.

SIN #7   Do Not Rehearse—Play It by Ear.

If there ever was a guaranteed formula for failure, this is it.

If you want to stumble, fumble, and sing off key, this is a sure way to do it. If that doesn't bother you, think of the audience. They deserve something better than an amateur reading a script, or trying to think up what he or she is going to say on the audience's time.

What is it that makes you think you can get by with what the pros would never try: performance without practice?

There is no fast-food line to giving a good presentation. Presenting is easy to learn but hard to do. As with most endeavors, you have to pay your dues. And that means rehearse, rehearse, rehearse.

If you can plead "not guilty" to the Seven Deadly Sins, you will be on your way to a winning performance. But to get the applause you deserve please don't get a ticket for any of the twelve most common mistakes in Figure 2A. More about them later.

MOST COMMON MISTAKES

1. Poor 1st impression

2. No objectives

3. Dull, dry, and boring

4. Frozen in one spot

5. Weak eye contact

6. Poor facial expression

7. No humor

8. Poor preparation

9. No audience involvement

10. No enthusiasm/conviction

11. Poor visual aids

12. Weak close

FIGURE 2A

Hot Drugs For Sweaty Palms

HOT DRUGS
FOR
SWEATY PALMS

1. MEMORIZE THE FIRST _____ MIN.

2. PREPLAN THE FIRST 3 to _____ WORDS.

3. CREATE _____ SHEETS.

4. R_____, RE_____, REH_____.

5. ARRIVE _____ HR. EARLY.

6. MEET, TOUCH AND T_____.

7. DEEP _____ GETS POISON OUT.

8. LIFT _____ ON CHAIR OR

9. PRESS _____ TOGETHER.

10. IMAGINE THEY'RE ALL _____ _____.

11. THE MIRACLE DRUG IS _____ FITNESS.

12. TAKE THE DALE _____ COURSE.

FIGURE 3A Guaranteed ways to dry up sweaty palms.

HOT DRUGS FOR SWEATY PALMS

It may start the night before your presentation. If not, then by the time the sun comes up on the big day you may start to get one or more of the diseases in Figure 3B.

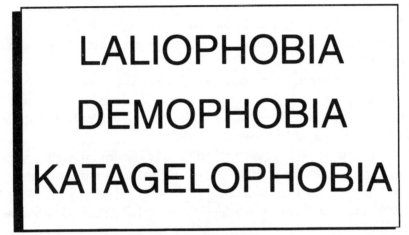

FIGURE 3B Speaking diseases

They are:

- Fear of speaking
- Fear of crowds
- Fear of ridicule

The symptoms are:

- Fast pulse
- Shallow breathing
- Muscle spasms that affect the
  —voice
  —knees
  —hands
- Dry mouth
- Cold extremities
- Eyes dilated

- Nausea
- Sweaty palms
- Tight nerves
- Blurred vision

You will be in very good company. Studies have shown that the number one fear of human beings in the United States is speaking before a group. In fact, the study revealed that people fear speaking before a group more than they fear death.

You may become obsessed with the greatest fear of all, best expressed by Roscoe Drummond when he observed, "The mind is a wonderful thing —it starts working the minute you're born and never stops until you get up to speak in public."

Don't be surprised if your mind starts wishing for laryngitis, a snowstorm, the flu, an earthquake, a closed airport, or anything that would cancel or postpone the presentation.

What's going on here is both good news and bad news. The bad news is, you will probably never get completely over it. The good news is that everybody has it—entertainers, professional actors, even people who conduct workshops on public speaking. The additional good news is that your presentation will be better because of it. Your mind will be quicker, your enthusiasm greater, your conviction stronger. Your

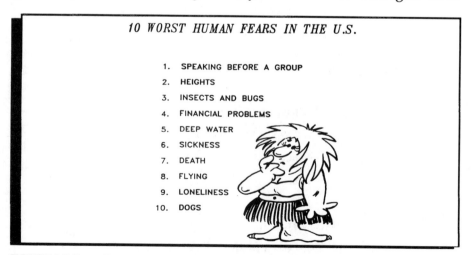

10 WORST HUMAN FEARS IN THE U.S.

1. SPEAKING BEFORE A GROUP
2. HEIGHTS
3. INSECTS AND BUGS
4. FINANCIAL PROBLEMS
5. DEEP WATER
6. SICKNESS
7. DEATH
8. FLYING
9. LONELINESS
10. DOGS

FIGURE 3C From The Book of Lists. People fear speaking before a group more than they fear death.

sweaty palms are your friends. They are proof positive that you are a normal human being. Normal because it's in your blood and in your genes. You inherited it from your earliest ancestors. Nature has given us the juice to fight or flee in threatening or uncomfortable situations. The juice is adrenaline, which automatically pumps into the blood-stream to help you out. So be glad you have it.

We need to understand that nervousness in front of a group is not a physical or psychological deficiency. It is a normal and healthy reaction of the body. It is nature's way of helping you be your best.

Professionals bet on nervous horses. Horse trainers know that nervous horses perform better.

If you feel like you're going to die when you stand up to talk, the good news is that throughout history there is not a single recorded death from stage fright. What we want to do is to get those butterflies to fly in formation.

Here's how.

#1   MEMORIZE THE FIRST *TWO* MINUTES

When are the sweaty palms the worst? When we start, in the middle, or at the end? When we start, of course. When do people get their first impression of us? When we start. Why couldn't they get it later on after we're settled down?—doesn't work that way. So what we want to do is out-fox the fright. We can do that by memorizing the first two minutes. Then we stand up we go to memory location "x," open our mouth and do a "memory dump." Two minutes later we'll be settled down and everything will be all right. We will have been on automatic pilot during the first critical 120 seconds. The worst worry is over. When the opening is over, the butterflies are in formation. And if you've done your homework in preparing an interesting and exciting opening (see Chapter 5) you're guaranteed to be on your way to an outstanding presentation.

#2   PREPLAN THE FIRST THREE TO FIVE WORDS

For your body chemistry and your personality, what are the most natural three to five words you would say first for every key point, every example, every story, etc.? The best way (some would say the only way) to win your audience over is to be who you are. Let them see and hear the real you. The way you would say something, describe something, or tell something is uniquely you. So decide in advance the first three to five words that are uniquely you for each key point you plan to make.

#3 CREATE CHEAT SHEETS

Guess what's going to be on the cheat sheets? You got it. The first three to five words you will say for each key item. More detailed information and examples of cheat sheets are coming at you in Chapter 10.

#4 REHEARSE, REHEARSE, REHEARSE

The single most effective thing you can do for sweaty palms is *rehearse.*. The second most effective thing you can do for sweaty palms is *rehearse.* Guess what the third thing is?

If you're not attracted by the carrot, maybe you're motivated by the stick. The stick is what will happen to you if you don't rehearse. The results are shown in Figure 3D.

#5 ARRIVE *ONE* HOUR EARLY

I promise you'll be glad you did. Murphy's Law will prevail. Whatever can be broken, missing, burned out, or forgotten will be. You will need at least one hour to get the ship in shape before you sail.

One hour will also give you enough time to do what the pros and presidents do—go to the front of the room, visualize the audience in their seats, and deliver your first two minutes. Then when the bell rings and they are really in their seats, you just do for the second time what you did the first.

There's another reason for arriving early. Some of the attendees will also arrive early. That gives you another opportunity to dry up those sweaty palms by following the suggestion in #6.

#6 MEET, TOUCH, AND TALK

We want to meet, touch, and talk with some of the early arrivals. Where are they from? What do they do? This has an amazing effect. When you stand up in front they are not an audience. They are warm, friendly

FIGURE 3D

people. They are not the enemy. They are people who are here because they want to be here. They want to hear what you have to say. The ones you've met, you liked, and they seemed to have liked you. So from the moment you stand up you are already among friends. But only if you've met and talked with them before the program starts. Don't go off by yourself. If you do, the only thing you will think about are weak knees, a squeaky voice, and shaky hands. And the more you think about it the worse it will get. Just the opposite happens when you force yourself to meet and talk with the people. You get your mind off of yourself and onto the people, As a by-product, you will pick up tidbits you can relate to or reference in your presentation.

The other side of this coin is that the people are interested in you. You are an expert on the subject you are going to talk about, but they also hope you are a regular guy or gal. They do not want you to be aloof, or distant, or act like an authority figure. They want you to be warm, friendly, and human. Don't disappoint them: "Reach out and touch someone."

The more you know about the audience and the more they know about you, the more at ease you both will feel. You will not be strangers but people who have come together for a slice of time to share a common interest.

#7 DEEP *BREATHING* GETS POISON OUT

If your heart beats fast and your nerves are tight and your palms a little sweaty—you're probably breathing out of the top one-third of your lungs. Guess what's collecting in the bottom two-thirds? Poison. And poison makes you break out in a cold sweat. So do some deep breathing and get the poison out.

#8 LIFT *UP* ON CHAIR

This tip alone is worth the price of the book. Here's what you do. While you are waiting to be introduced, reach out and down on each side and grab the bottom of the seat of the chair you're sitting in. Pull up hard for five seconds. Then repeat, repeat, repeat. What you're doing, of course, is releasing tension.

If you have a table in front of you, you can extend both arms under the table, palms up, and press up for five seconds.

If you don't have a table and you're not sitting in a chair, then move right along to #9.

#9 PRESS *PALMS* TOGETHER

In fact, if you practice pressing your palms together, you can be doing it during your presentation and they won't even notice.

#10 IMAGINE THEY'RE ALL *STARK* N_____

This one is "X-rated," but it works wonders. So if you're a little uptight just look out at the audience and imagine they're all sitting there stark naked. You'll be amazed at what a calming effect it will have. See some nice scenery, too.

#11 THE MIRACLE DRUG IS *PHYSICAL* FITNESS

If all else fails you can take the miracle drug of the decade—physical fitness. The only thing that's better for controlling nerves and anxiety is preparation and rehearsal. So if you've been on the fence and need another straw on the camel's back to persuade you to shape up, here it is. Remember that business of no free lunch, or you can pay me now or pay me later? Well, you can work it out the day before or sweat it out while you're on the stage. The voice of experience says that if you jog three miles the morning of your presentation, you'll have no problem with the jitters.

I discovered a substitute trick one morning in Peoria. A howling blizzard kept me off the streets—I couldn't do my three miles. The trick? A fast walk up and down ten flights of stairs in the hotel. Do that six or eight times and you'll get the same good results, and you won't have to go out in the snow.

Do not—I repeat, *do not*—take mind-changing or mood-altering drugs for your nerves. They create a deceptive illusion. You will think you are doing better but you will be doing worse. And worse than worse, you could find yourself on a one-way street going to a dead end.

#12   TAKE THE DALE CARNEGIE COURSE

How would you like to make 30% more money each and every year than the guy or gal sitting next to you? If you're in the marketing game you can, you know. Take the Dale Carnegie Course. (In which, by the way, I have no financial interest of any kind.)

But if you say to me, "I'm too sophisticated for that kind of rah-rah stuff," let me give you a few references.

Reference #1. Call Rome and ask to speak to the Pope. Ask the Pope, when he took the Dale Carnegie Course, how it helped him get ahead in his line of work.

Or if you want someone closer to home, call Detroit and ask for Lee Iacocca. Ask Lee how, when he took the Dale Carnegie Course, it helped him become the most admired businessman in the world.

Or ladies, call Dallas and ask to speak to Mary Kay. And ask Mary Kay, when she took the Dale Carnegie Course, how it helped her become the owner of more pink Cadillacs than anybody else in the world.

If the cost of the Dale Carnegie Course is a little heavy for you, there's another answer that's almost (not quite, but almost) free. Join Toast-masters. If you're the busy type you'll be glad to know that they meet morning, noon, or night. They're all over the world and probably less away or even in your own building. Check them out in your local phone book. You'll be glad you did. After all, what is it you're doing right now that's more important than an investment in your financial future?

Another answer is to attend a presentations workshop. They come in different sizes and shapes. Some are better than others. The most important variable is the experience, credentials, and abilities of the instructor. A second important consideration is whether the focus is strictly on platform and delivery skills, or does it also consider the content and effectiveness of accomplishing an objective. You should also ask, "What do I walk away with that I can use today?"

In summary, if you keep your mind occupied with other people and positive thoughts, there will be no room for sweaty palms.

- You know ten to 20 times more about the subject than anyone in the room.
- They are here because they want to be here.
- They like you and want you to succeed.
- You are well-prepared.
- Your presentation is well-organized and thoughtfully constructed.
- You have memorized a well-thought-out opening.
- Your visual aids are well-designed and will enhance your presentation.
- You have a solid case and a strong close.
- The audience is open-minded and receptive to new ideas.

More good news. You are never as nervous as you think you are. I can prove it. In my two-day workshop we videotape the presentations. People are always amazed at how calm they look on the outside compared to the way the feel on the inside. So even though you are shaking like a leaf on the inside, you're probably solid as a rock on the outside.

Design The Close First

Great is the art of beginning, but greater the art is of ending.
                    Henry Wadsworth Longfellow

The most important part of the presentation is the close. It is at the close where you either accomplish your objective, or you don't. Do they believe? Do they agree? Will they commit? Will they act? Will they order? The answers to these questions tell you how well you accomplished your objective. The objective is a statement at the beginning—the audience gives you their answer at the end.

You have only one chance at a professional close. So important is the close, that we plan it and design it from the very beginning. We want the objective and the close to dictate the contents of the entire presentation.

Remember when we were kids how we would focus the sun's rays with a magnifying glass onto a piece of paper, and burn a hole in it? Same with our presentation. Everything we say and do in the opening and the body should complement, concentrate, and focus on our close. This will provide singleness of purpose and keep our eyes on the target. The contents of the close will dictate the contents of the body. We begin a presentation where the audience *is*, but we close the presentation with where we want them *to be*. The close is our destination.

Let's look at it from the audience's point of view. It is at the close where they hear what they came to hear. Everything up to now has been in support of the close. We have been making our case, providing the evidence, and proving our points. Now we are ready to deliver the package, gift wrapped, with a red bow.

We want to use the trial lawyer's technique called the doctrine of primacy and recency. The doctrine of primacy says lead off with your strongest statement. The recency argument says finish with your biggest blast.

They will remember best what they hear last. So when it's all over and the people are leaving, what is it that you want them to have in their heads?

This technique is the same as that used by some writers of mystery novels. They conceive the ending first, then work backward to develop the rest of the story.

You might think the close is obvious and easy. I suggest to you that this is not the case. The secret is to leave the audience wishing for more, while at the same time feeling good because they got more than they expected.

You should write out the last two minutes of the presentation, and then do what the pros do—memorize it. That's right, memorize it. (What are you doing that is more important than giving this audience the very best you've got to give?) If you had just two minutes to tell someone the bottom line of your entire presentation, what would you say? That requires some planning and heavy thinking. Your entire presentation is no better than the close. So do it right. Take a tip from Broadway—the best song is the last song. Have them leaving singing your song.

When you write out your close, be sure you write it the way you talk, and not the way you write. It has to sound like you—not like Hemingway.

There are two other reasons for having a well thought out, written, memorized, and rehearsed close. The day will come (usually soon) when you will either not have enough time or will run out of time. When that happens, you can just skip to the close. Usually the audience will not even be aware that you have left out some of the presentation.

The second reason is that the day will come when someone important will say to you, "For heavens sake, if you have something important to tell me, start at the end." You'll be ready. Give them your two-minute close.

The worst possible close is one that just peters out and sinks into the sunset with the comment, "Well, that's about all I have, folks. Are there any questions?"

How many times have you sat through a presentation and, when it was all over, wondered what the main message was?

What about questions at the end? The problem is, this is the high point of your entire presentation—this is the climax. If you now enter into a prolonged Q-&-A period, you will detract from your close, bore most of the audience, and quickly lose the enthusiasm of the group. Moreover, it's completely unnecessary. If you plan a Q-&-A as part of the presentation, there will be no questions at the close. They will all have been answered.

An entire chapter on questions and answers is coming up. For now, let's remember that the time to not only answer questions, but also ask questions, is *during* the presentation, not at the end of the presentation.

In summary, the good news is this: If you have a strong opening and dynamite close, the stuff in the middle can be mediocre and you will still have a good presentation.

Let's take a look at some examples of closes:

THE HAPPY ENDING CLOSE

Here is an example of an approach that we might call the Happy Ending Close.

Let's suppose that we are selling or promoting a product or service that we will call "X." We structure the presentation so that in the opening we present:

- The *characteristics* of an ideal "X" or
- The criteria for selecting the best "X" or
- The functions of a comprehensive "X."

In the body, we talk about the *functions, features, benefits, and advantages* of our "X."

Then in the close we summarize the *strengths* of our "X."

Guess what? Our strengths turn out to be exactly the same as:

- The characteristics of an ideal "X" or
- The criteria for selecting the best "X" or
- The functions of a comprehensive "X."

The key to the Happy Ending Close is to design the close first. Having done that, you back up to the opening and structure it to be exactly compatible with what you now know the close will be. Or simply put, the close provides the perfect answers to the questions raised in the opening. The only way you can make that happen is to design the close first. If you don't, you may raise questions in the opening for which you have weak answers, or no answers in the close.

If you use this approach properly then you can ask for and get the audience's agreement on key points in the opening. If they agree with the opening, then the close becomes a "gotcha."

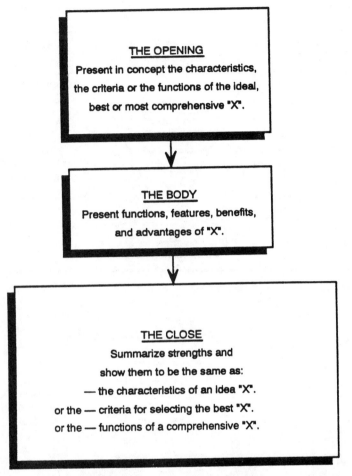

FIGURE 4A The Happy Ending Close.

THE FUNNEL CLOSE

Here's another approach. Let's suppose you have a total of 15 key points in your presentation. The day after the presentation, how many of the key points do you think people will remember? That's right. Not very many. Maybe three or four. And they may not be the three or four we would prefer them to remember. After all, he who emphasizes everything, emphasizes nothing.

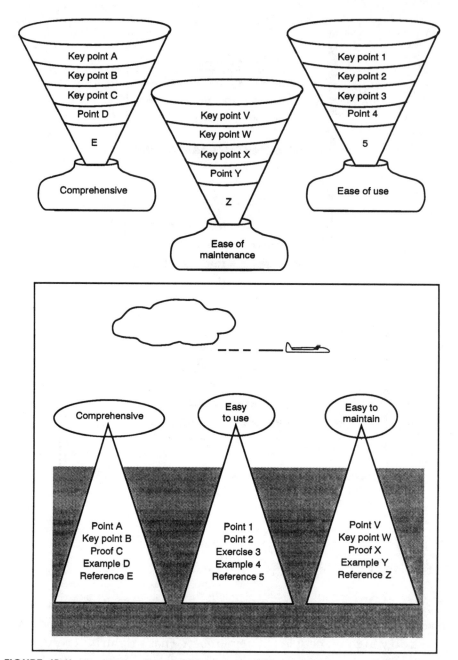

FIGURE 4B If we use the Funnel Close we can control what the audience will remember. A variation of the Funnel Close is the Iceberg Close.

Suppose we approach the subject another way. Let's start with the day after and make the assumption that they will remember three things. If that's the case then what are the three things we would like them to remember? These will be the three things our close will focus on.

Suppose we conclude that the three things we would like the audience to remember is that our product or service is:

1. Comprehensive

2. Easy to use

3. Easy to maintain

Now we can design the close around these three central thoughts. We classify each of the 15 key points within the three central thoughts.

Our close can now be represented pictorially by three funnels as shown in Figure 4B.

THE ICEBERG CLOSE

Having established the close, we can now back into the opening and the body to provide a logical structure and flow to the presentation.

What we have done is to categorize 15 independent key points into three summary conclusions that we want the audience to remember.

The point of this structure is that even though people will not remember the 15 supporting key ideas, they will remember that the proof of each of the three central thoughts was convincing, and at the time they heard it they understood and agreed with it.

So even though they forget the details, they will remember the three truths you want them to retain. And it doesn't matter whether the subject is a computer, an investment program, or a lawn mower.

THE SHOTGUN CLOSE

Well, you say, that sure makes a lot of sense. I like the structure, the flow, and the logic. However, the nature of my presentation doesn't lend itself

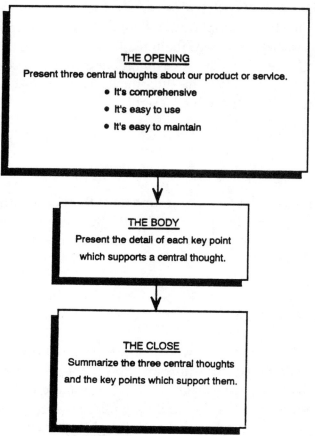

FIGURE 4C The Iceberg Close.

to that structure. I have many key points to make and they aren't well related, so they don't fit into your funnels. In fact, they are almost the opposite of a funnel—they are more like a shotgun.

Suppose for example, you are in personnel or training. Your job is to give a company orientation presentation to new employees. You have 20 unrelated key points to present.

How in the world are you going to get them to remember 20 key points? Here's how you do it. We call it the Shotgun Close.

HOW GOOD IS YOUR INVESTMENT IQ?

True or False

1. T F   Out of every 100 people, 26% are flat broke at age 65.

2. T F   40% of all people living in poverty are women.

3. T F   The cheapest way to borrow money is to use the method that will discount interest.

4. T F   Baron de Rothchild said, "Common stocks are the 8th wonder of the world."

5. T F   The technical method of forecasting future stock movement is correct only 75% of the time.

6. T F   Persistent pattern in the stock market occur as frequently as 75% of the time.

7. T F   The greater the risk — the lower the commissions a stockbroker gets.

8. T F   70% of all stockbrokers own mostly over-the-counter stocks — not Blue Chips.

9. T F   10% of all people who invest in the stock market over 10 years do not make money.

10. T F   Of the Forbes 400 richest men and women in America, over one half made their fortune in the stock market.

11. T F   Mark Twain said, "July is the most dangerous month to speculate in stocks."

12. T F   Stocks recommended on Wall Street Week have typically outper-formed the market average by 5-10% within the next two months.

13. T F   The five year performance of mutual funds has been significantly greater than the market average.

14. T F   The size and scope of the large institutional investor gives them a significant advantage over the individual investor.

15. T F   If you had followed Howard Ruff's advice over the last five years, you would have had an average annual return of 24%.

16. T F   Professional investment advice has been wrong 25% of the time.

17. T F   There are more millionaires per capita in Maine than any other state.

18. T F   Solid investment advice for the last 20 years would have been to buy good stocks and hold on to them.

19. T F   Over the last five years you would have done better in Old Master Paintings than anything else.

20. T F   You can defer taxes — but never avoid them completely.

FIGURE 4D The Shotgun Close. Creative questions can get attention, keep interest, and provide a format for the presentation.

The secrets to success of the Shotgun Close are:

1. Repetition

2. Verbal participation

3. Written participation

We design the close to be in the form of a verbal test that we all take together. The test consists of multiple questions—one for each key point. Figure 4D is an example of a Shotgun Close.

Again, having now designed the close, we can back up to the opening and the body.

This approach is not only different, it is also stimulating, interesting, and is the best way for an audience to remember a large number of points.

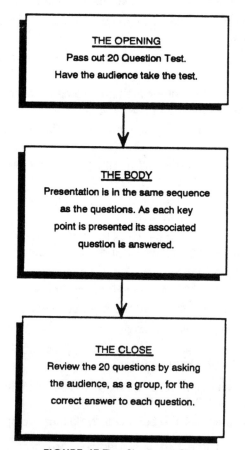

FIGURE 4E The Shotgun Close.

You should think through each question carefully to make it interesting and provocative. Also, provide space on the handout for the audience to write down the correct answers.

This technique uses the wisdom of K'ung Futzu from 479 B.C. (his English name is Confucius):

- *They hear it.*
- *They see it*—if you have proper visual aids.
- *They do it*—by the act of writing the correct answer.

Built into the structure of the presentation is

1. Repetition
   a. Seen at the beginning
   b. Elaborated on during the presentation
   c. Reviewed at the close
2. Participation
   a. Each individual takes the test during the opening.
   b. The answers are written on the handout as they are covered in the presentation.
   c. The group retakes the test verbally during the close.

They won't remember the 20 questions. But any time one of the 20 questions is asked, they will remember the answer.

By the way, the answer to all 20 questions is False.

THE "I'M HERE TO HELP" CLOSE

Here's another approach called the "I'm Here To Help" Close. Suppose we have a picture of the close that looks like Figure 4G.

Now we can back up to the opening and body.

CLIENT OBJECTIVES	HOW I CAN HELP	FEATURE OF MY PRODUCT OR SERVICE
Increase productivity	A._____	1._____
Reduce cost	B._____ C._____	2._____ 3._____
Improve service	D._____ E._____ F._____	4._____ 5._____ 6._____

FIGURE 4F "I'm Here to Help" Close.

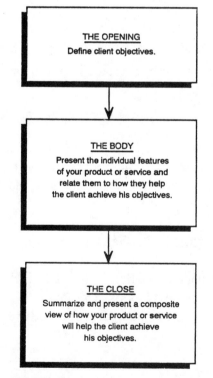

FIGURE 4G "I'm Here to Help" Close.

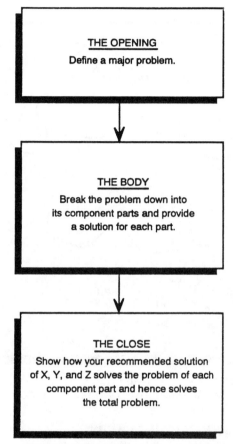

FIGURE 4H The Jigsaw Puzzle Close.

THE JIGSAW PUZZLE CLOSE

Next we have a close called the Jigsaw Puzzle Close.

Here we have in our mind the image of a close that looks like Figure 4H.

The idea is that we define a major problem, then break the problem down into its component parts (the seven pieces of the puzzle). We then provide a solution (X, Y, or Z) for each component part of the problem.

The purpose of the close is to show that all component parts of the problem are solved by our recommendation of X, Y, and Z.

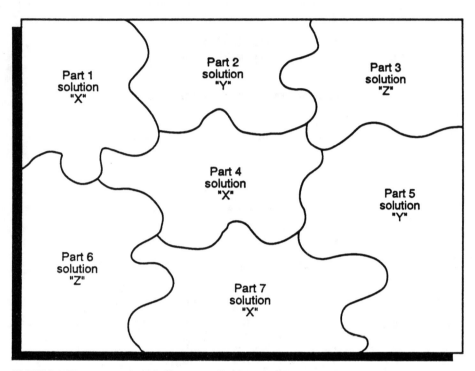

FIGURE 41 The Jigsaw Puzzle Close. Define a problem. Break it into parts. Show that all parts are solved by our recommendation of X, Y, and Z.

PREDICTIONS OF THE FUTURE CLOSE

Here is a popular close. You almost can't lose with this one. You simply predict what's going to happen in the future.

People like good news. If you are predicting the future, you can make the news as good as you want. And the farther out the prediction, the more plausible it may seem. Also, this type of close gives you an aura of wisdom and insight that is rare among mortal beings.

If our close is Predictions of the Future, then we can back up to the opening and the body.

THE HOW GREAT IT'S GONNA BE CLOSE

A variation of the Predictions of the Future Close is one that closes with a word picture of how great it's gonna be. First we describe how bad it

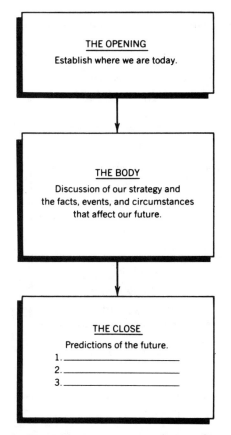

FIGURE 4J Predictions of the Future Close.

is now. Then we present our recommendation. The close paints a picture of money, fame, glory, peace, freedom, productivity, etc. as a result of buying our product or implementing our recommendation.

The trick here is to construct the closing word picture first. Then we can back up to the opening and describe how bad the current situation is in regard to each element we describe in the close.

THE BRIDGE OVER TROUBLED WATERS CLOSE

Another approach is the Bridge Over Troubled Waters Close.

The idea here is that we define a goal that the audience would like to achieve. The problem is that there are major obstacles to achieving this

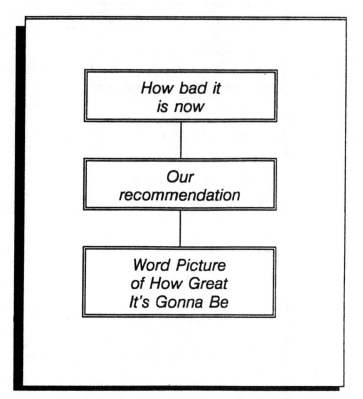

FIGURE 4K The How Great It's Gonna Be Close.

goal. These are shark-infested waters. There is danger, risk, and uncertainty in achieving our goal. The odds of the audience making it alive with their health intact are not good. Fortunately, your firm provides a bridge over these troubled waters that will allow them to safely cross over to the other side and get the pot of gold at the end of the rainbow.

THE TEN COMMANDMENTS CLOSE

Figure 4M is the close I use for my one-day Executive Selling Skills Seminar. It combines:

- The attention-getting gimmick of the Ten Commandments
- A one sentence summary of the major concepts along with a carrot and a stick for each
- A fill-in-the-blanks exercise

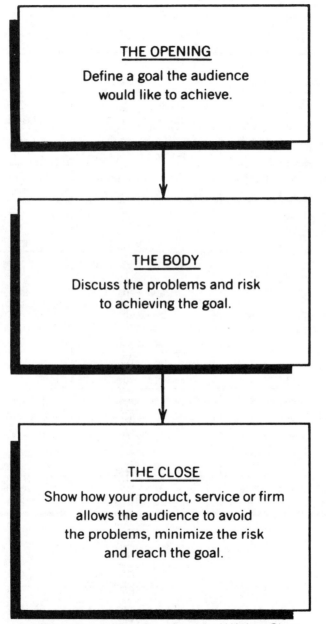

THE OPENING

Define a goal the audience
would like to achieve.

THE BODY

Discuss the problems and risk
to achieving the goal.

THE CLOSE

Show how your product, service or firm
allows the audience to avoid
the problems, minimize the risk
and reach the goal.

FIGURE 4L The Bridge Over Troubled Waters Close.

Executive Selling Skills

THE 10 COMMANDMENTS	IF YOU DO	IF YOU DON'T
1. Thou shalt call at the ____.	Selling is easier/quicker.	Selling is harder/longer.
2. Thou shalt identify _____ _____.	Market to human beings	Selling in the dark
3. Thou shalt spend ½ day at the CIA.	Focus on the customer's business	Focus on products
4. Thou shalt determine the CSF's.	Solving business issues	Selling functions and features
5. Thou shalt know your customer's _____.	Give the customer what they want	Selling product performance
6. Thou shalt know the buyer's _____.	Be compatible and likable	Sound like a salesman
7. Thou shalt appeal to the pathos.	Provide answers to personal needs	Selling a commodity
8. Thou shalt appeal to the ethos.	Build relationships and partnerships	Have a lack of trust and confidence
9. Thy customer's _____ shall be thine own.	Act like a partner	Act like a vendor
10. Thou shalt use the **Breakthrough Strategy**	Answer an urgent need	Selling pie in the sky

Thou Shalt Begin It _____.

FIGURE 4M

Answers to Figure 4M:

1. Top 2. Decision Makers 3. CIA = Public Library 4. CSF = Critical Sucess Factors 5. goals 6. chemistry 7. Pathos = emotion 8. Ethos = trust/confidence 9. enemy 10. Breakthrough Strategy = a small decision that will result in a rewarding experience as a direct result of your intervention.

THE AUTHORITATIVE QUOTE CLOSE

Another idea for a close is to build it around some authoritative quotation which is in direct support of your objective.

For example, listen to this close.

"And now, in summary and in conclusion, let me tell you the John Ruskin story. Does anyone know who John Ruskin was? He's dead, you know. He died almost 100 years ago. He was a real ugly fellow, too. (Show a transparency picture of John Ruskin.) One of the ugliest fellows I've ever seen. Why are we talking about John Ruskin? We're talking about John Ruskin because you often quote something he wrote. There's hardly a week goes by that you don't quote John Ruskin.

"But when you quote him, you quote the shorthand version of something he wrote. The shorthand version you quote says, 'There ain't no free lunch.' But I want to show you the longhand version of 'There ain't no free lunch'—the way he originally wrote it (show transparency of John Ruskin quote), and then I'll have a footnote for you."

Footnote: "And so in conclusion I say to you: beware of (show Beware of Bargains transparency) bargains in:

parachutes,

life preservers,

fire extinguishers,

brain surgery,

and computers."

To tailor this to your audience, simply change the word "computer" to your product or service, or to the profession or occupation of your audience.

Other examples of authoritative quotes might be:

Some men see things as they are, and ask "Why?" I dare to dream of things that never were, and ask—why not?

George Bernard Shaw

To a group of personnel people:

When you hire people smarter than you are, you prove that you are smarter than they are.

R. H. Rand

For a public service presentation:

No man can truly help another man without helping himself.

Ralph Waldo Emerson

I shall pass this way but once.
Any good that I can do
Any kindness I can show
To any human being
Let me do it now
Let me not defer nor neglect
For I shall not pass this way again.

William Penn

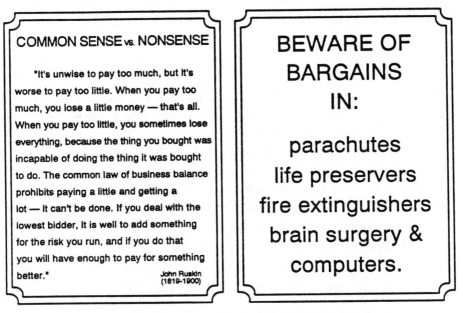

FIGURE 4N The Authoritative Quote Closer.

Or how about this attention-getting play on words:

There are two kinds of failures; those who thought and never did, and those who did and never thought.

John Charles Salak

If you don't have your own book of quotations, your local librarian can fix you right up.

THE EMOTIONAL CLOSE

Remember, Aristotle said that it is not enough to appeal to reason and logic. He said we must also appeal to the emotions. So don't be bashful about putting emotion into your close.

Here is my close to IBM dealers and distributors.

"And so in summary and in closing I say to you: I love you, I want you, I need you, I can't get to where I want to go without you. And I believe in you. I believe the power within you and the support behind you are infinitely greater than the task before you.

"So come along with me. Let's walk this road together. And I believe, I believe, I believe you will walk the road to Glory."

You can even integrate audience participation and music into your close. Here is my close to an IBM sales rally.

> And so I say to you,
> It's morning in America,
> And it's sunrise at IBM,
> So look across the valley.
> The sun is shining.
> The grass is green.
> The corn is as high as an elephant's eye,
> And out yonder the moose is loose
> And colored blue.
> Everything's gonna be all right.
> And now I ask you—*Do you see the light?*
> Say "I see the light."
> *Do you believe?*
> Say "I believe."
> And so I have a vision of the future.
> I hear the music playing.
> (Start the music—"When the Saints Go Marching In")

It's playing "When the Saints Go Marching In,"

But the words are different.

They say:

Oh, When Big Blue Goes Marching On

Oh, When Big Blue Goes Marching On

Oh Lord, I Want to Be In That Number

When Big Blue Goes Marching On.

Here is an example of a close for a personal development or management development presentation. This one has a little bit of everything—logic, emotion, quotes, and audience participation.

And so if you want to soar with the eagles,

And not walk with the turkeys,

I'm talking to you.

If you want more fame in your future than you had in

your past,

I'm talking to you.

Where you are today is the result of choices you made

yesterday.

But where you will be tomorrow

Will be the result of decisions

You will make today.

The greatest of the German philosophers said:

"Whatever you can do, or dream you can,

Begin it.

Boldness has genius, power, and magic in it."

Shakespeare said a similar thing:

"There is a tide in the affairs of men,

> Which, taken at the flood, leads on to fortune;
>
> Omitted, all the voyage of their life
>
> Is bound in shallows and in miseries."

The choice is yours.

Let's all take the final exam together.

There are only three questions.

The answers are one word each.

The only person I can change is _____.

The only day I can start is _____.

The only time I can make the decision is _____.

Other sources of a close are personal experiences of yourself or of someone with whom the audience would recognize or identify. These must relate and tie-in to your closing theme. They are most effective when they paint a picture of the following:

From failure to success

From depression to elation

From weakness to strength

From poor to rich

From sick to strong

From defeat to victory

From the bottom of the heap to the top of the mountain

You get the idea. And if the punch line can be told with an Alfred Hitchcock closing style—they'll never forget it.

IT'S SHOWTIME

THE OPENING

You never get a second chance to make a first impression.

Just as we tend to judge a book by its cover, so your audience will come to an opinion of you in about two minutes.

Other than the close, the opening is the most important part of the presentation.

SHOULD WE START ON TIME?

The first and most obvious thing people will notice is whether the meeting starts on time. What are you going to do? Here it is time to start and only half the people are present. So we should wait another five or ten minutes, right? Wrong. The first rule is: The meeting starts on time, if you're in charge of the meeting. What's the big deal about waiting a few minutes? ("Everybody does it.")

Let's look at it this way. What do you think is going through the minds of the people who were there at 9:00 and the meeting finally starts at 9:20? Something like, "My time is as valuable as yours—if you were going to start the meeting at 9:20, why didn't you announce it for 9:20? The next time you schedule a meeting for 9:00 do you think I will be there at 9:00? Not on your life." In fact that's probably the very reason half the people weren't present at 9:00 for this meeting.

By the way, how long would you guess the ten-minute coffee break is going to last? And when you announce that the meeting will reconvene after lunch at around 1:00, when do you think you will really start? Well, you get the idea—we bring it on ourselves.

An exception to the start-on-time rule would be a selling situation where the key decision maker is late. In that case, the show doesn't start until the king or queen is seated.

YOUR INTRODUCTION

Write your own. Don't leave it to chance or to the imagination of the program chairman. If you do, the probability is 90% that you'll be sad you did. Your introduction is too important to be wrong, boring, and too long. Take charge and control the content by handing the chairperson a typed introduction. And please, write it in plain English.

If your company is like others, introductions tend to be stereotyped. After awhile they all sound alike: full of acronyms, strange sounding titles, and job descriptions that most people never heard of and care little about. The only titles that really get people's attention are:

President of_____

Inventor of_____

The first man to_____

Discoverer of_____

Author of_____

Winner of_____

And so on.

If you have one of those handles, you've got it made. If you don't, let me suggest a change of pace. Something so radically different from most bios that it will catch the audience completely off guard, and give them a warm feeling about you before you even open your mouth.

The centerpiece is human interest. A natural human question is, "I wonder what he or she is really like?" So forget the wordy titles and meaningless job descriptions. Delve back into your past and put together a human interest bio. No one but you has been where you've been, done what you've done, and had your experiences. Let them hear the uniqueness that is yours alone. If you do it right, I promise you it will bring a smile to their faces and warmth to their hearts.

Be sure your bio includes the answers to these four questions:

1. Why this speaker?
2. Why this subject?
3. Why this time?
4. Why this audience?

And finally the toughest job of all—keep it short. How short? You're not going to believe this. The correct answer is 120 words or 60 seconds—whichever comes first. And remember, the greater the person, the shorter the introduction. The President of the United States is introduced with the first six words in this sentence.

IF YOU ARE INTRODUCING YOURSELF

If you are introducing yourself, the one thing you must convey to the audience is your credibility in the subject matter you are going to present. But we need to be careful because in the mind of the audience there is a fine line between establishing credibility and being boastful, cocky, or worst of all, arrogant.

Don't cross the line.

Here is how we handle it. Say just enough to lay the foundation of credibility. The additional details that might sound boastful we will build into the presentation at strategic points as references, or as examples to punctuate a key point. We just include them as key word notes on our cheat sheets.

HOW TO INTRODUCE THE AUDIENCE

Depending on the type of meeting you are part of, you might want to go around the room and have each person introduce themselves and give a little personal information such as name, what they do, and where they come from.

I always disliked these introductions because it always seemed like the person just in front of me was a natural born comedian who was full of humor, wit, and clever remarks. I would follow her with a mundane name, rank, and serial number.

Here is an idea for getting around that problem if the audience comes from different organizations. It also has the effect of getting people to know each other and warms up the crowd. Have each person interview the person sitting beside them. You provide a format for the interview by passing out the interview form in Figure 5A.

After a few minutes the teams reverse roles and the interviewee becomes the interviewer. Each person then introduces to the group the individual they interviewed by providing the answer to at least five of the questions on the interview form. It's a lot of fun, and loosens up the audience. A good icebreaker.

It also provides you, the presenter, with some valuable information about the audience mixed in with the levity. This is information you need to do three things:

<u>**ANSWER ANY 5 OF THE FOLLOWING**</u>

1. COMPANY, DEPARTMENT OR CITY _____.
2. EVERY NEW YEAR'S EVE YOU RESOLVE _____.
3. YOU HAVE ALWAYS WANTED TO _____.
4. YOUR'RE A SUCKER FOR _____.
5. IN HIGH SCHOOL YOU WERE KNOWN AS _____.
6. YOUR VERY FIRST JOB WAS _____.
7. THE ONE THING YOU'VE LEARNED IS _____.
8. THE BEST PART OF YOUR JOB IS _____.
9. THE WORST PART OF YOUR JOB IS _____.
10. YOUR GREATEST ACHIEVEMENT WAS _____.
11. YOUR FAVORITE ACTOR/ACTRESS IS _____.
12. YOUR SPOUSE THINKS YOU'RE _____.
13. MOST PEOPLE DON'T KNOW THAT YOU _____.
14. IN ADDITION TO WORK, YOU'RE ALSO GOOD AT _____.
15. THE BEST MOVIE YOU EVER SAW WAS _____.
16. IF YOU COULD DO IT ALL OVER YOU WOULD _____.
17. THE BEST BOOK YOU EVER READ WAS _____.
18. YOUR FAVORITE FOOD IS _____.

FIGURE 5A

1. Level-set the audience.

2. Tailor the presentation.

3. Set the level of expectation.

LEVEL-SET THE AUDIENCE

What is this level-set the audience business? This refers to the different levels of knowledge and experience on the part of the audience about the subject. To the extent that you have a great variance you run the risk of boring some of the people and confusing others. What we should do is pick a base level for the start of the presentation. If we set this level higher than the knowledge level of some of the people, then we need to bring them up to the base level.

We do this by identifying the key points of the premise, which become the base level, and reviewing these points briefly and in summary form. One effective technique for accomplishing this is to put these points in the form of questions that you address to the group. This will not only level-set the group, it will also let those who have little or no knowledge know in a dramatic way that the premise is well-known and accepted.

TAILOR THE PRESENTATION TO THE AUDIENCE

We tailor the presentation by learning as much as possible about our audience in advance of the meeting. In the introductions you will pick up additional information for the tailoring of the presentation to the audience. The introduction technique also affords you the opportunity to add real-time spice to both your opening and the close. Here's how. Have a pen or pencil handy during the introductions. As certain information comes to light during the introductions that you can relate and tie in to the content of the opening, make a note of it and the name of the individual linked to it. Then in your opening refer to that person by name and the subject of his or her comment.

For example, suppose Joe Smith says, ". . . and I'm here because I need help in so and so." Then in your opening you can say, "And Joe, I'm pleased to tell you that we are going to cover so and so in great detail. In fact, by the time we finish, you will. . . ."

Then at the close, guess what? That's right. We refer to Joe and his comment again—perhaps with a direct question such as: "And in summary, Joe, have these key points helped you with so and so?" Well, of course he will say yes. And you've already got a testimonial.

That kind of personalization adds spice, and breathes life and spontaneity into your presentation.

In the final analysis, our objective is to tailor the presentation to the interest of the group. The first opportunity we have to do that is in the opening. You will be amazed at the effect minor modifications will have on the initial audience perception—even though you're using an off the shelf or canned pitch.

Speaking of tailoring and effective openings, let me tell you one of the most clever things I have ever seen in my life.

I used to run a class for new managers at IBM. Its purpose was to give them management exposure to the company and provide them with information on management philosophy, rules of the road, and Dos and Don'ts. To accomplish this we had guest presenters representing key functional areas of the business.

One of the key areas was personnel. To present this we had the manager of personnel. Well, this guy was an absolute master at tailoring a presentation to an audience. Let me explain.

If you think about it and put yourself in the place of a new manager, there are certain obvious subjects you want to know about and will have questions about in the area of personnel. Things like merit pay increases, appraisals, how to handle the poor performer, and so on.

This guy had given this presentation so many times that he knew there were always eight to ten subjects that new managers would like to discuss. And they were always the same eight or ten subjects. He had a prepared presentation on each of these subjects.

So in his opening, rather than introducing the subjects he was going to talk about, he would walk up to a blank flip-chart stand, and ask the audience what they would like to talk about in the area of personnel management. As subjects were volunteered from the floor he would write them on the flip chart. Guess what? They were always the same eight or ten subjects. The only difference was the sequence. He had the material for each subject in a manila folder. He just rearranged the sequence of the folders, and began presenting the subject on the flip chart.

I saw him do this many times. It never failed. He always presented the same subjects. He was always giving the same presentation he had planned to give, anyway—just in a different sequence.

The impact on the audience was dramatic. Not only was he talking about what they wanted to talk about, but they were dumbfounded at his in-depth knowledge and statistical quotes about what appeared to be spontaneously volunteered and unrehearsed subjects.

There is another type of tailoring we need to think about.

If you are one of multiple presenters on a program, you need to understand what came before you and what's coming after you. If you do, then you will be able to tie-in to material that has already been covered and refer to things that are yet to come.

Again, you can create the perception that your presentation was specifically designed to fit right here, and to complement the other presentations.

There is nothing worse than finding out after the fact that 50% of your material was covered by the previous speaker, or, even worse, that you flat out contradicted the previous speaker and with no explanation.

So if you can, sit in on the other presentations—at least the one just preceding yours. If you can't do that, try to get a detailed briefing in advance from the host.

SET THE LEVEL OF EXPECTATIONS

Finally, with or without introductions, we need to set the expectation level of the audience. This needs to be communicated as part of the statement of objective of the presentation. The audience needs to know what they will get out of it. We must avoid the kind of situation where the audience thinks the presentation is about saving on taxes while the thrust of your presentation is on financial planning and strategy. This is nothing more than the simple rule of tell them what you're going to tell them. We want no Alfred Hitchcock endings.

Here, for example, is how I set my expectations for my Executive Selling Skills Seminar.

"Do I have all the answers? No, of course not. Do I have all the right answers? Probably not. Have I brought some killer bees that you can unleash on the enemy? No, I haven't. Do I have a miracle drug that will send you to the Golden Circle? No, I don't. What I do have are proven principles and marketing techniques that have stood the test of time. All of you will know some of them. Some of you will know all of them. They are based on experience, not on opinion. You may differ with my conclusions because your experience may be different from mine. But that's 100% all right, for selling is not a science, and there is no patent on persuasion."

HOW TO OPEN YOUR PRESENTATION

You are an unknown quantity for only 120 seconds. After that, everything you say will be heard in the context of the impression from your first two minutes. Your most listened-to sentence is your first sentence. Therefore, your opening deserves careful preparation and your very best thinking.

In the first 120 seconds you must:

- Capture their attention and interest
- Answer the question "What's in it for me?"

The audience must understand a selfish reason to pay attention to what you have to say.

If you cannot articulate a selfish reason for the audience to pay attention to what you have to say, then you have nothing to say to this audience.

The best example I have ever heard of someone explaining to me why it was in my best interest to pay attention happened in Texas.

I was going through jet fighter pilot training. Before they strap the stove pipe on you, you have to go to ground school to learn the electrical system, the fuel system, and so on. One day the instructor walked into class and held up a red ribbon with a pin at the end. He said, "Gentlemen, do you know what this is?" Well, of course we didn't know what it was.

He explained that this was the safety pin from the ejection seat of an F-86 Saber Jet, and that for the next hour he was going to lecture to us on how to eject from an F-86 Saber Jet and survive. Then when we finished the lecture we were going out that door to the parade grounds where there was an actual ejection seat mounted on a vertical railroad track. And, one at a time we were each going to be strapped into that seat. We would pull down our visors, pull up the left arm rest, pull up the right arm rest, then pull the trigger underneath the right arm rest—and when we did, a live 20 millimeter cannon shell was going to explode under our you-know-what, and we were going to be shot straight up.

Do you think he had our attention? Let me tell you, every man in that room could have given that lecture. That instructor had explained very well a selfish reason for us to pay attention to what he had to say.

So early in the opening be sure you answer these kinds of questions.

Why are we here?

Why is it important?

What's in it for me?

How can I use it?

What will I get out of it?

People will pay attention and listen to what you have to say if they can see an advantage to themselves. The advantages can take many forms:

Material gain
Management approval
Prestige
Self-advancement
Imitation of others
Social approval
Self-satisfaction
Sense of accomplishment
Peace of mind
Satisfy curiosity

Here are some ideas for attention-getting openings.

- Ask a provocative question
  "How many of you own a foreign car, camera, or watch?"
- Use a quote that relates to your subject
  "The best way to help the poor is not to be one of them."
  "The duration of the marriage is inversely proportional to the cost of the wedding."
- State a startling fact or statistic (see Figure 5B)
- Appeal to human interest (see Figure 5C)
- Tell a story or personal experience that relates to your subject. A side benefit of telling a story is its value in overcoming nervousness in the first two minutes. You will be the most natural, the most animated, and speak with the greatest conviction and enthusiasm when you are relating a personal experience.
- Refer to a recent, well known event or local newsworthy story—and bring the local paper with you.
- Pay a sincere compliment to the audience's organization, their company, their profession, etc. And if you can relate something in your background to the common denominator that brings them together, you will get a double-whammy benefit of "I am one of you and we're all in this together."

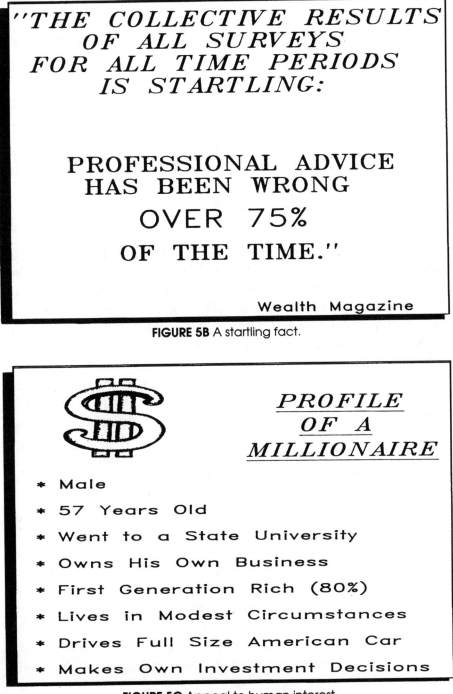

"THE COLLECTIVE RESULTS OF ALL SURVEYS FOR ALL TIME PERIODS IS STARTLING:

PROFESSIONAL ADVICE HAS BEEN WRONG OVER 75% OF THE TIME."

Wealth Magazine

FIGURE 5B A startling fact.

PROFILE OF A MILLIONAIRE

* Male
* 57 Years Old
* Went to a State University
* Owns His Own Business
* First Generation Rich (80%)
* Lives in Modest Circumstances
* Drives Full Size American Car
* Makes Own Investment Decisions

FIGURE 5C Appeal to human interest.

HERE'S WHAT NOT TO DO

- Don't tell a joke unless you are naturally humorous and it relates directly to your subject.
- Don't give dictionary definitions of words.
- Don't say, "Thank you, Mr./Ms. Chairperson, I am honored to address the _____." (Sounds stereotyped and insincere.)

- Don't think small. Instead, think big. Small thinking does not stir the imagination of great men.
- Don't apologize for anything.

Now we come to the single most important thing you can do to ensure a successful opening and a good first impression. *Memorize the first two minutes.* To do that you will have to write out the words in advance—think about them, modify them, get them just right for you. Then when you stand up and start and the anxiety level is at its highest, you don't have to think up what you're going to say. Just turn the brain switch to automatic and out it comes.

The alternative is not very attractive. In fact, it's kind of scary. The alternative is trying to think up what you're going to say, and create a good first impression, while your sweaty palms are at their worst.

Simple solution—*memorize the first two minutes.*

Do not—repeat—*do not* take the first five or ten minutes to cover administrative detail. Remember, other than the close, the opening is the most important part of the presentation. Don't blow it with a downer. Spread those administrative details out during the day or cover them after the opening, not before.

Speaking of Don'ts, if you hand out an agenda or show an agenda on a visual, just show the subject names. Do not show the start and stop time for each subject. If you do, the audience will be preoccupied with time, the schedule, and where you are in the program. If you get behind schedule, they will think you did a poor job of planning.

If you are ahead of schedule, they may think you are leaving something out and not giving them 100 cents on the dollar. You can't win so don't try.

Getting Attention And Keeping Interest

When we stand up to tell our story, one of the first things we need to do is answer the question that's in the mind of the audience. The question is always there but it is never asked. We must answer the unasked question. That question is "What's in it for me?" If you cannot articulate a selfish reason for the audience to pay attention to what you have to say—then you have nothing to say to that audience. As you can see in Figure 6A, there's a plug in the jug, and your presentation is not going to get into your audience's head until you answer the unasked question. If you want to tilt the odds in your favor, be sure to include a few words like the following in your answer:

Sex

Money

Safe

Control

Unique

Opportunity

Trouble

Weight

Enjoyment

Pain

Health

Time

Comfort

Fame

Glory

Popular

Family

Profit

Fear

Love

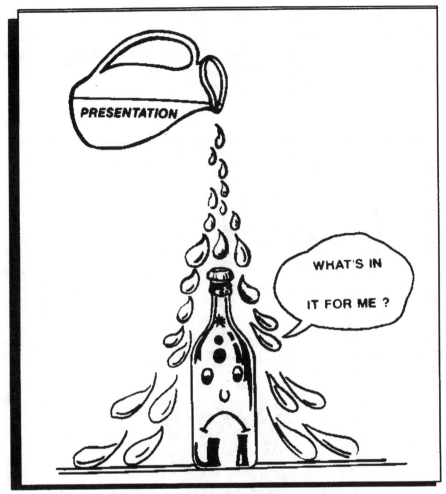

FIGURE 6A You must answer the question.

When you answer the unasked question, that gets the plug out of the jug. Now, you would think that your presentation would go into his or her head—and some of it does.

But look at what's happening in Figure 6B. Most of it is spilling out onto the floor. Why is that? Well, it simply has to do with the way we are. Most people speak at the rate of 120 to 200 words per minute. But the human mind can comprehend at the rate of 600 words per minute. So there are a lot of idle cycles. What happens during the idle cycles? The mind branches out to the beach, the bar, the band, the boys, the girls—doesn't get an "interrupt signal," forgets to come back, and your presentation spills out onto the floor.

FIGURE 6B It's hard to keep the interest of the audience.

The Northwestern School of Speech reports that the attention span of an audience is approximately nine seconds. If we drew a diagram of what was happening it would look like Figure 6C.

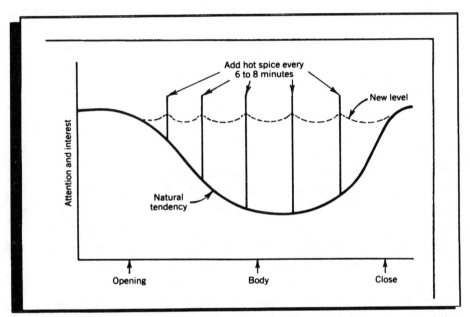

FIGURE 6C Attention and interest tend to decline during the body of the presentation.

Almost always the attention and interest level are high at the beginning of a presentation. So the good news is, you've got a free ride for the first few minutes. The bad news is, if you blow the first few minutes, you're a dead duck for the rest of the hour—or the rest of the day. The audience is checking you out: "Is this going to be worth listening to? Is he or she any good?," or "I wish I had sat in the back near the door so I could sneak out."

But it is difficult to maintain that high level of attention and interest. The natural tendency as we move into the body of the presentation is for the attention and interest to decline.

But what happens when presenters get near the end of the presentation? Do they ever give us a hint that they are about to finish? Do they ever say words like:

"in summary"

"in conclusion"

"to wrap this up"

"for my last_____"

Yes. Almost always they tell us they are about to finish. What do you think happens to the level of attention and interest when the audience hears the words "in summary?" You got it. It zooms back up: "Wake up, Joe, it's about over."

Our problem is that we have lost the attention and interest of the audience in the body of the presentation. What we need is a shot of Hot Spice every six to eight minutes in the body of the presentation. This would have the effect of raising the average attention level. One technique to accomplish this is common among those who make their living with their mouth: politicians. If you listen carefully, you will hear politicians use the phrase "in summary" or "in conclusion" multiple times in their speeches. Is that a mistake? Absolutely not. The politicians know exactly what they are doing, as every six to eight minutes they use the phrase "in summary." What happens to the attention level when the audience hears the words "in summary?"

We can learn from the politicians by planning a "peak" or a touch of Hot Spice every six to eight minutes to our presentation. The effect is to create a funnel, as shown in Figure 6D.

Now almost all of the presentation is going into his or her head. We see in figure 6D examples of things we can use every six to eight minutes to raise the attention level. Interesting visual aids, humor, questions, eye contact, proper use of the voice, good body language, movement, enthusiasm, war stories, and such all add interest to the presentation.

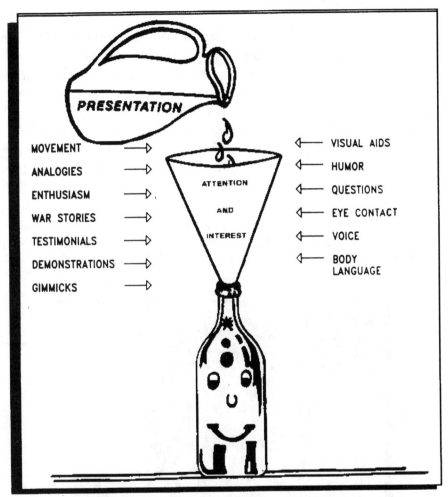

MOVEMENT

ANALOGIES

ENTHUSIASM

WAR STORIES

TESTIMONIALS

DEMONSTRATIONS

GIMMICKS

VISUAL AIDS

HUMOR

QUESTIONS

EYE CONTACT

VOICE

BODY LANGUAGE

FIGURE 6D When you add Hot Spice, you create a funnel.

Giving an effective presentation is more of an art than a science. So we should use some industrial showmanship to keep their interest and attention. Your brilliant insights, sound arguments, and startling revelations will fall on deaf ears if their minds are out to the beach. Good content alone is no assurance of an effective presentation. And *great* content never saved a bad delivery.

Let's talk about some techniques and examples of industrial showmanship to get their attention and keep their interest.

GOOD VISUAL AIDS

Of the total inventory of information you have in your head, 75% came to you visually, thirteen percent through hearing, and a total of twelve percent through smell, taste, and touch. Now let me ask you a question. Of the total inventory of information you have in your head, what percentage came to you through hearing?

When I say that in front of a live audience there is a long silence, even though I just told them the answer three seconds before. Occasionally, I will get one or two delayed and feeble answers of thirteen percent.

Suppose, instead, I showed them a picture (Figure 6E) and then asked the same question.

Note the difference between saying the words and seeing a picture. We know from studies that have been done that your audience will forget 75% or more of what you *say* in 24 hours or less.

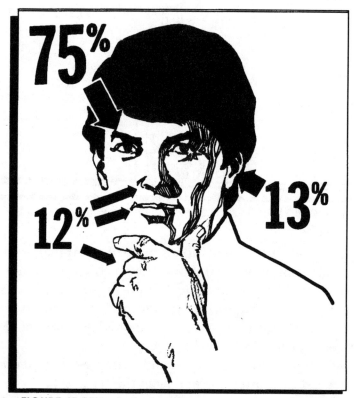

FIGURE 6E 75% of what we know came to us visually.

Here is a trick I use at conventions or conferences where I am the speaker on the second day. Scares me to death every time I do it, but it's never failed yet. I remind the attendees that the first speaker, just 24 hours ago, talked for 32 minutes. I then say, "If you could remember just 25% of what they said, then you could talk for eight minutes on that subject. Would anybody like to volunteer to talk for eight minutes on what that speaker said?" There is a dead silence. I then ask, "Does anybody even remember the speaker's name?" I never cease to be amazed at the silence, followed by laughter.

If we draw a diagram of comprehension and retention, it would look like Figure 6F.

Heraclitus said, "Eyes are more accurate witnesses than ears." And Alfred Lord Tennyson reminds us, "Things seen are mightier than things heard."

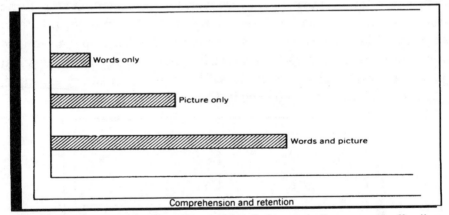

FIGURE 6F Words and pictures used together are six times more effective than words alone.

If I show you a picture, the comprehension and retention is three and a half times greater than just saying words. If I both show you the picture and give you the words that go with the music, the comprehension and retention is six times greater than just saying the words.

Homer said, "The mind is more slowly stirred by the ear than by the eye."

We remember:

10% of what we read

20% of what we hear

30% of what we see

50% of what we both see and hear

We can apply some common sense tests to this. Which do we remember best—faces or names? Faces of course. The image of the face gets in our brain through the eyes. The names get in our brain through the ears. Or have you ever tried to explain something complicated to somebody who is having trouble understanding? Then there's a breakthrough and she gets it, and says, "Oh, I get the *picture.*" Have you ever heard anybody say, "Oh, I get the words?"

We have all heard that one picture is worth a thousand words. If that's true, then one picture is worth eight minutes of talking (at 120 wpm).

Good visual aids stimulate interest. They clarify, substantiate, and reinforce what has been said. Moreover, when presenting something new, the audience has no way of referring to a mental image of something they have never seen before. Just try describing a camel to someone who has never seen a camel. In fact, there are some things that are almost impossible to explain without visual aids. For example, "How many squares do you see in Figure 6G?

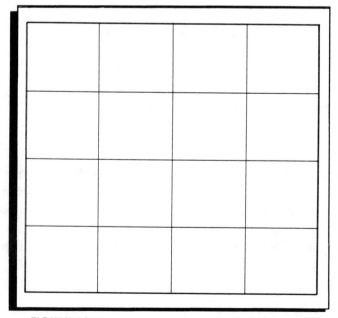

FIGURE 6G How many squares do you see—16.

Most people would say 16. But we could prove that there are actually 30 squares if we used a visual aid like Figure 6H.

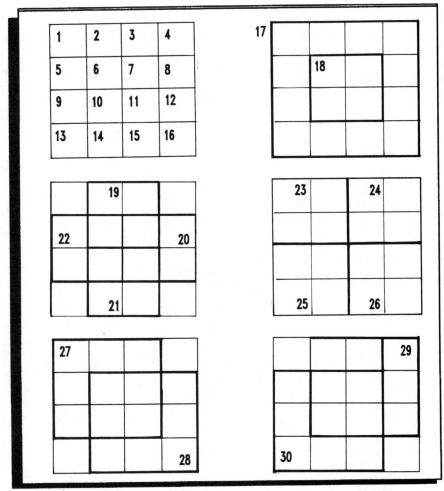

FIGURE 6H A good visual would prove there are 30 squares.

Visual aids have been effective since they were first used by a man who came down from a mountain carrying two stones tablets with ten rules on them.

BUT THERE ARE GOOD AND BAD VISUAL AIDS

The good and bad of visual aids are best described by example. Figure 6I is an example of a bad visual aid. If your visuals look like that, don't bother to dress for success because your visuals are designed for failure.

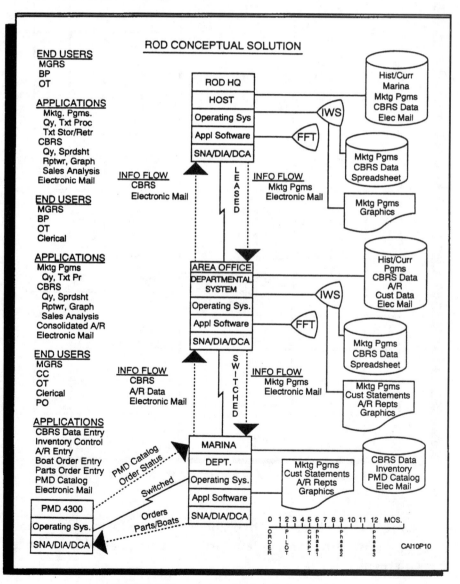

FIGURE 6I Example of a bad visual aid.

We lose business because we complicate our products and services, and we confuse our customers and our clients. We need to simplify, simplify, simplify. Let me give you an example. Look at the top half of Figure 6J. You might think that it looks like computer talk. It's not. I got that from a sales brochure (I said a *sales* brochure) of an insurance company. It describes an insurance product called Single Premium Variable Life. It would take me at least 20 minutes to explain that concept to you. If, however, I were to simplify it as shown in the bottom half of Figure 6J, I could explain it to you—not in 20 minutes but in ten seconds.

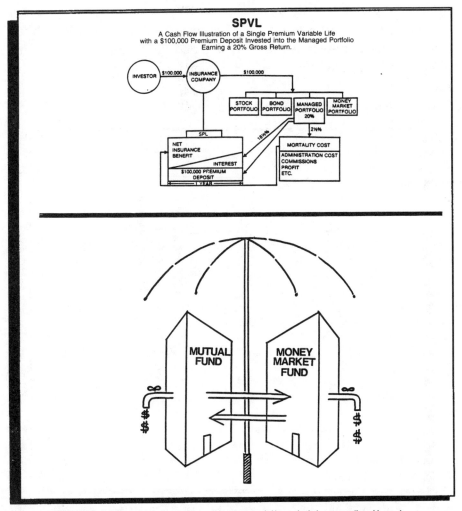

FIGURE 6J The wrong way (top) and the right way (bottom).

Let's see: "Let's take the tax shelter provided for the tax laws for the insurance industry. And under an umbrella of that tax shelter we set up a mutual fund and a money market fund—allow you to invest in either one, switch back and forth at any time—and take your money out on either side." A ten-second explanation of a complex subject.

And now I ask you, which is more likely to be understood? Which is more likely to be remembered and, more importantly, which is more likely to achieve my desired objective?

Simpler is better. Lincoln's Gettysburg address was 262 words, 202 of them one-syllable; John 3:16 is 26 words, 21 of them one-syllable. Simpler is better.

There is one simpler rule for a good visual aid. It should look like a billboard on an interestate highway that people are going to read going by at 65 miles per hour. If you make them look like that, you'll have it just right.

Take a look at Figure 6K.

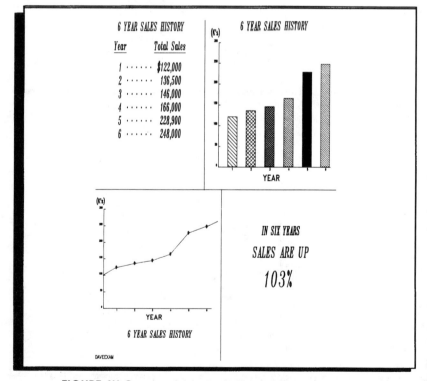

FIGURE 6K One bad (upper left) and three good.

The upper left is an example of what not to do. The other three examples are the right way. Or to do even better, take a look at Figure 6L.

FIGURE 6L Even better.

And please don't make a visual out of a full page of printing like Figure 6M. Instead, net it out like Figure 6N. Or even better, how about Figure 6O.

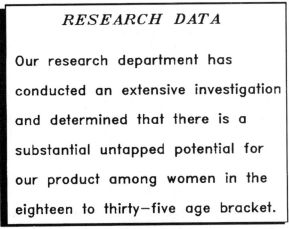

FIGURE 6M Bad.

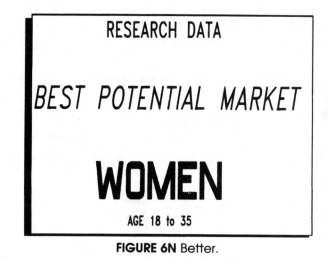

FIGURE 6N Better.

FIGURE 6O Best.

If your visual aids are in color, you will have an 85% higher attention span. Would you invite your neighbor over to watch the Super Bowl on a black-and-white TV set? Then why would we give black-and-white presentations to important customers and clients?

The combined use of pictures, symbols, and key words create an effective visual aid. Bar charts (either horizontal or vertical) are good for showing comparisons. Pie charts are good for showing the relationship of parts to a whole. Graphs are good for showing changes and trends over time. Diagrams are a good way to show complex structures or ideas.

Visual aids are even more effective in a presentation if you have a mix of charts, graphs, cartoons, bullets, and overlays. It's particularly important in long presentations.

We suggest earlier that you not use visual aids that consist of complete sentences. Remember, the purpose of the visual is to support the explanation, not to give the explanation. Moreover, written material on visuals has the characteristic of poor retention. This is because reading is not really a visual aid. It is more like "hearing through the eyes." People will tend to remember the visual layout, not the message it contains. For example, they will remember that there was a bold heading and four subpoints, but not the content. Visual aids are most effective when they are *visual* in *impact* rather than verbal.

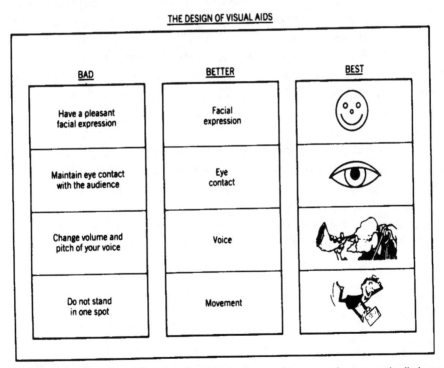

FIGURE 6P Here we see the contrast between using a sentence, a bullet, or a picture as a visual aid.

If you are using words, use them in bullet form, not complete sentences. This gives the presenter the chance to elaborate on each point. The bullet word or words would then be an aid to the presenter.

Now we come to a deadly sin. Once you have been hooked on visual aids, the tendency is to reduce the entire presentation to a series of visuals. But they lose their effectiveness if you rely solely on them to get your message across. The more visuals you use the less impact any of them will have. The tendency is to have too many. That causes Sin #6 of the Seven Deadly Sins (i.e., "Read verbatim every word on every visual"). It's better to have too few than too many.

It's important that your visuals be neat, attractive, and have a professional appearance. But they don't have to be master works of art. In fact, it's better if they aren't. If they have a super slick Madison Avenue look, it can suggest that the presentation was put together for a mass audience of anonymous people. A presentation that has a touch of home conveys the impression that it was put together specifically for that audience, and tailored just to them. If you would like some free professional help on creating colorful and exciting visual aid call 1-800-328-1371. That's the world headquarters of the 3M Company, the world's largest manufacturer and distributor of visual aid supplies. They'll tell you the name, address, and phone number of the 3M distributor in your city. Ask them, "What is the date and time of your next *free* half day workshop on creating colorful and exciting visual aids?" It's well worth your time since your visual aids have three times more impact than your words. (P.S. I have no financial interest of any kind in the 3M Company).

We conclude this section by reviewing some of the rules of the road of visual aids. The first three are the most important.

Keep it simple.

Keep it simple.

Keep it simple.

No more than three curves on a graph. One or two are better.

Use color. At least two, but no more than three.

Have one and only one key point per visual. There is one exception: If the information is familiar to the audience, you can combine a number of points.

Don't have a page full of numbers.

Translate complex numbers into pie charts, bar charts, or graphs.

Don't use complete sentences or paragraphs. Bullets only, please.

Ask yourself this question: Can the audience quickly and easily grasp what they see?

Use overlays for complex points.

The world's worst visual aid is a black-and-white transparency of a typewritten page.

Don't forget actual objects—the best visual aid is the real thing.

If you can't have the real thing, have a picture of it.

Make heavy use of pictures, graphs, and symbols.

Finally, let's not get so bogged down in the trees that we fail to see the forest. That's my way of saying that the greatest visual aid of all is YOU.

HUMOR

Of all the spice there is to use, the hottest spice of all is humor. Trouble is, very few of us are naturally humorous.

If someone who is not humorous tries to tell a joke, can you sense that it is awkward and unnatural? Yes, you really can. So the first rule of humor is don't tell jokes if it's not natural and comfortable.

There should be no doubt in your mind whether or not you are humorous. If you are, you know it very well. In fact, you have known it for years. It is obvious to both yourself and to the people around you. If there is any doubt in your mind, the answer is, you aren't.

The only thing worse than telling an awkward, unnatural joke is to tell a long, drawn-out awkward and unnatural joke. And yet, presenters do it all the time.

Even the professional comedians back off from the long jokes. They learned long ago that the one-liner is best of all.

I know you've seen it many times. The speaker walks to the podium, whips out a prepared speech (which he didn't write), and proceeds to read, with a monotone voice and a solemn expression on his face, how excited he is to be here. (More about nonverbal expression later). The very next thing he does is read a joke. And not just any joke. It's a long joke.

Worse still, the joke has nothing whatsoever to do with the subjext at hand. Which leads us to the second rule of humor: The humor must be relevant to the subject of the presentation. It's difficult enough for the audience to retain what you've said. Unrelated humor makes it worse. But natural humor that is directly related to the subject of the presentation will greatly enhance the material, its understanding, and its retention.

What do we do if we are uncomfortable telling jokes? Here's the answer: We tell stories on ourselves. Think back into your past. What we are looking for are situations, incidents, events, happenings, and experiences that at the time may have been embarrassing, stupid, or humiliating. Humor is tragedy separated by time and space. When you tell that incident or that experience you will tell it naturally, tell it with conviction, and tell it enthusiastically because it actually happened to you. So don't tell artifical jokes—tell the truth as it happened to you. Be sure it's related to the point of the presentation you are trying to make.

There is an important and powerful by-product of telling stories on yourself. It enhances the audience's positive perception of you. People who tell stories on themselves are good people. Just be sure your stories are in the embarrassing category and not the boastful category. Otherwise, you'll get the opposite effect. All of us have embarrassing stories we can tell on ourselves. And remember, 'tis a poor storyteller who cannot enhance a good story.

For example: Many years ago when I was going through jet fighter pilot training I was assigned to a pilot training base in Big Spring, Texas. The base has since been closed and only the oldtimers remember that it was even there. Recently I was making a presentation in Texas. In the course of my remarks I mentioned that I had spent many months in Big Spring, Texas. At the end of the presentation the host came up to me and suggested that I should have explained what I was doing in Big Spring, Texas, since the only thing the audience knew about Big Spring was that it had an insane asylum and a prison—and they were wondering which one I had spent the many months in.

When I'm giving my corporate strategy presentation, I tell the story about my first visit to IBM corporate headquarters. I tell them that the thing that stood out most in my mind, more than anything else, was the color of the carpet.

"You would never guess the color of the carpet in IBM corporate headquarters. You would think it would be a pretty blue. But no. It's orange. That's right—orange. And not a pretty orange. It looks to me like the color of orange that would glow in the dark. I turned to the guy who was showing me around and said, 'Who in the world picked out this carpet?' He said, 'the President.'

"I immediately replied, 'Sure is pretty, isn't it?'"

Well, every time I tell that story to an IBM audience, it brings the house down.

Another way you can use humor is to capitalize on predictable things that will happen during a presentation. For example, it is predictable that one or more people will arrive late, that is, after you've started. If it fits your chemistry and your personality, you can use this as an opportunity for light humor. Think up and plan in advance what you would say, for instance "Come right in. Are you the one who does the time management lecture?" or "Come on in, I'm sorry we started early."

Of course, what you say not only needs to fit your personality but also the audience and its mood.

Another example: If you use transparencies without frames, it is predictable that sooner or later one of the transparencies will start floating and moving in some direction while laying on top of the projector. Knowing this, you can plan what you are going to say when this happens, such as

"This subject is so hot it's hard to keep it in one spot."

"In spite of what you see, this is not a flaky, floating idea."

"This is so dynamic that it's moving, even as we sit here."

"This offer won't last long because it's on the move."

Another way to create humor is through the use of visual aids that have a built-in humor.

From birth to age 18, a girl needs good parents.
From 18 to 35, she needs good looks.
From 35 to 55, she needs a good personality.
From 55 on, she needs good cash.

Sophie Tucker, 1953

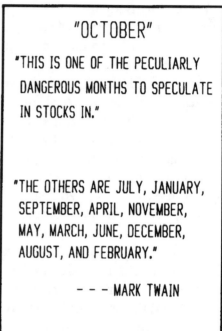

"OCTOBER"

"THIS IS ONE OF THE PECULIARLY DANGEROUS MONTHS TO SPECULATE IN STOCKS IN."

"THE OTHERS ARE JULY, JANUARY, SEPTEMBER, APRIL, NOVEMBER, MAY, MARCH, JUNE, DECEMBER, AUGUST, AND FEBRUARY."

– – – MARK TWAIN

FIGURE 6Q Cartoons that relate to the subject are excellent sources of humor.

FIGURE 6R So are quotes.

EYE CONTACT

Have you been in one of those meetings where the presenter is looking at the floor, the ceiling, or out into space with a glazed look?

We speak to people through our eyes. Don't handicap yourself. Look at the audience. More specifically, look directly at one person in the audience for three to five seconds.

Here's how. Before you speak the next sentence or thought, lock in on a specific person and hold that eye contact until you have completed that phrase or that thought. Careful now—not too long, because eye contact can turn into a stare and that can be intimidating.

If you have tent cards, name plates, or if you know the people or some of them, use their names as you speak to them.

If you do these two simple things—make eye contact and use their names—I promise you, you will have no problem getting attention and keeping interest.

The best use of this technique I've ever seen is by the professors at the Harvard Business School. They will look at every person in the room multiple times and call them by name. And every person there thinks, "He's talking just to me." And he is—for those five seconds.

Let me tell you about a hidden danger. It happens to me all the time. In a typical audience, there will be a few people who have big smiles on their faces and nod their heads yes to everything you say. Guess what the natural human tendency is? That's right, to look only at these people who are smiling and nodding yes.

Here's a story that illustrates the effect smiles from the audience can have on the presenter. At a university a particular professor had the annoying habit of racing back and forth across the front of the classroom. In this particular class, a large percentage of the students were from the same fraternity. They put together a plan back at the house. Here's what they did. When the professor reached a specific spot in his racing in front of the class, they would all smile. When he moved away from that spot they would all stop smiling. Well, before that class was over, guess where the professor ended up standing? You got it— exactly on the spot where he got a lot of smiles.

There's a bonus for you if you concentrate on eye contact. It keeps you from turning your back on the audience and reading from a screen, a board, or a flip chart. You can't read a script *and* have eye contact with the audience. So lift up your head, smile, and look 'em in the eye.

VOICE

The first rule of the voice is to be heard. But don't confuse being heard with effective communications.

The single biggest problem with the voice is the tendency to speak in a monotone. And, in fact, if you are reading a script it's hard not to talk in a monotone. It takes a conscious effort to vary the volume, tone, and pitch of the voice.

A common mistake is to assume that all one has to do is speak in a loud voice. But an hour of loud monotone quickly becomes an hour of loud noise. In fact, just to illustrate the contrast, I have heard a 90-minute presentation made in a whisper. It was amazing. You could hear a pin drop. Everyone in the room was sitting on the edges of their seats, thinking at any moment the presenter was going to reveal the secret of the universe. An observer turned to me and said, "Did you know that people will believe anything if you whisper it?"

An effective use of the voice is the change of pace. Speak rapidly for a few seconds, pause, return to a normal pace, then speak rapidly again. The words per minute will average out to be the same as if you had spoken in a monotone, but what a difference. The master of this technique is Paul Harvey. In fact, if you want a free lesson on the use of the voice, just listen to the network anchorperson on the evening news.

The antidote for the monotone is a mix of conviction, enthusiasm, confidence, desire, and rehearsal. Take a swig of that before you start, and you'll be in fine shape.

MOVEMENT

There is a psychological barrier that separates you from your audience. It's a line that runs across the front of the room—it's like a wall. It creates the atmosphere of me/they, of we/them. It's like the offense versus the defense. It's an adversarial relationship.

You need to break down that barrier—and it's easy to do. Just walk across the line occasionally. That says, "I'm one of you"; "I'm on your side"; "We're all in this together." Just a few steps forward into the audience will do it. If you're on a stage or a riser it's even more important to break the barrier by stepping down to ground level for a minute or two. If that's not practical, the least you can do is walk to the front of the stage.

Never underestimate the power of nonverbal communication. Use it to your advantage. What you *do* speaks louder than what you *say*. Walk across the line.

Be a triple-threat presenter. Have three positions, not one. The only thing worse than standing in one spot for an entire presentatioin is to be a racehorse running back and forth across the front of the room. That's a terrible distraction.

Here's the game plan. Position #1 is the home position for the mainstream part of your presentation. Position #2 is for the alternative media you will use to change the pace, add emphasis, and give the illusion of spontaneity. Decide in advance which material will be the mainstream media, and which will be the alternative. Use the alternative media at least once every ten minutes.

Now in every presentation there are several places where you will elaborate in some detail on some point or concept. For some of these, you will know the subject so well and the words will flow so smoothly that you will have no need to refer to notes. That's the time to cross the line and break the barrier of the wall. That's position #3. Again, decide in advance specifically when and where you will do this. Then rehearse. And do it the same way every time.

ANALOGIES

The way our minds work, we are better at understanding and remembering pictures and symbols than we are at remembering words. For example, when someone says the word *car*, our mind flashes up a mental picture of an actual car, not the English letters C-A-R. If I say *ice cream*, what image comes to your mind? I bet it's not the letters of the alphabet.

The world's best communicators use analogies to create easy-to-understand images of their key points or concepts. So let's take a lesson from the pros. You can communicate concepts in less time, with better understanding, and with longer retention if you use analogies. They are so effective that people will remember some of them all their lives.

Have you ever seen a ski instructor teaching children how to ski? To tell them how to slow down or stop, the instructor will say, "Make a snowplow with your skis." Or if they happen to be from the South where they have never seen a snowplow, the instructor will say, "Make a slice of pizza with your skis."

To teach them how to turn, the instructor might say, "Let's pretend that our knees are the headlights on a car. When a car turns, the headlights turn. Now place your hands on the headlights (knees). To turn to the right we simply turn the headlights (hands on knees) to the right, and so on."

Effective presenting is simply a matter of communicating the picture you have in your mind to the mind of another person. The more complex the material or concept, the more important it is to use analogies and word pictures. And the simpler, the better.

For example, let's say that I'm talking to the president of a company about a computer. One way I might describe my computer would be to say, "Mr. President, this computer has a storage capacity of two and a half billion bytes, a 16 millisecond access time, and a transfer rate of three million bytes per second." What does that mean to the president of a company? Nothing.

Suppose instead I said, "Mr. President, this computer can store the entire Encyclopedia Britannica in 20 languages, access any piece in any language in less time than it takes to blink your eye, then read it at the rate of one volume every two seconds."

Or, what if I were trying to explain the national debt, which is four trillion dollars. How much is four trillion dollars? Nobody knows. Suppose I said that if you had four trillion dollars you would have enough money to send every child in the U.S. to Harvard for one year, send every adult to Club Med in Bora Bora, French Polynesia for two weeks, give every homeowner a free full size, in-ground concrete swimming pool, and still have one trillion dollars left over?

Or see what you think of this. Would you take a trip on an airplane if there were four major plane crashes every day with 250 people aboard each plane and all were killed? That's how many people die prematurely every day from smoking cigarettes.

There are few things more powerful and more memorable than an analogy.

If you have trouble coming up with an analogy to explain some abstract concept, just explain it as best you can to your next-door neighbor, then ask her what it reminds her of. You will also find that barbers, bartenders, and taxi drivers will often come up with an analogy.

THE REVELATION TECHNIQUE

To a large extent, if I can control what you see, I can control what you think.

The other side of the coin is, if I don't control what you see, then I lose control over what you think. For example, if I flash Figure 6T on a screen, and begin to discuss the first item, your eyes and your mind are reading ahead. You are not hearing what I'm saying about the first item because you are already halfway down the page.

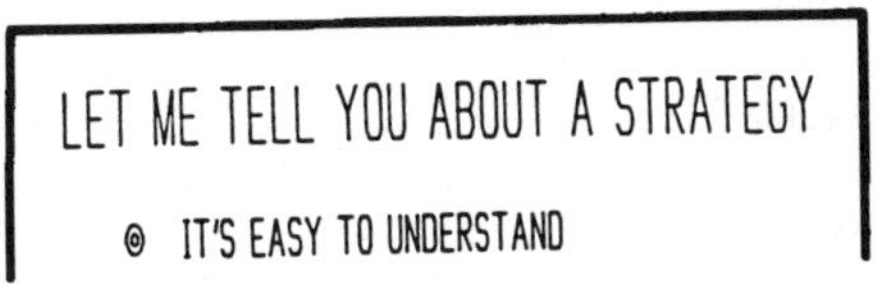

LET ME TELL YOU ABOUT A STRATEGY

⊙ IT'S EASY TO UNDERSTAND

LET ME TELL YOU ABOUT A STRATEGY

⊙ IT'S EASY TO UNDERSTAND

⊙ IT'S SIMPLE TO IMPLEMENT

⊙ IT PROVIDES INSTANT LIQUIDITY

⊙ IT REQUIRES LESS THAN ONE HOUR PER WEEK

⊙ ALL ACTIVITY IS CONDUCTED BY PHONE

⊙ YOU NEVER PAY SALES COMMISION

⊙ IT'S IDEAL FOR IRA'S OR KEOGH PLANS

⊙ IT DOES NOT REQUIRE YOU TO PREDICT, FORECAST, OR GUESS THE FUTURE

⊙ IT MAKES MONEY IN GOOD TIMES AND IN BAD TIMES

⊙ IT IS LOW RISK – HIGH REWARD

FIGURE 6S The revelation technique allows me to control your thinking by controlling your seeing.

FIGURE 6T Here I have lost control over what you are seeing and hence what you are thinking.

As a presenter, I must not let that happen. I want you to read the item halfway down the page only when I am ready to talk about it.

The way I control this is the revelation technique. Let's suppose I am using an overhead projector. Using a blank piece of paper I simply cover up the transparency, revealing the items one at a time as I discuss them, as in Figure 6S.

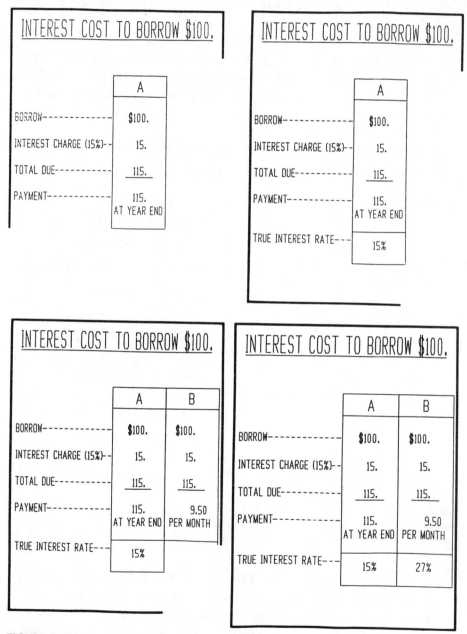

FIGURE 6U The revelation technique can be used to reveal a little at a time or a lot at a time.

Variations of this technique are effective for a step-by-step explanation of a concept. Figure 6U illustrates a four-step revelation to explain true interest rates. Please note, this is not a series of overlays—it is simply covering up with blank paper what you do not want to reveal until you are ready to talk about it. This allows you to control the attention and focus the thought process through a series of logical steps to a conclusion.

The final transparency without this technique would be confusing and difficult to explain. You would have no control over which part of the transparency your audience is looking at and what they are thinking. Certainly you would lose the element of surprise.

NUMBERS AND STATISTICS

A sure way to lose the attention and interest of your audience is to start showing a bunch of numbers and statistics. And yet many times these numbers are the very foundation of the key point you are trying to make.

What to do?

The difference between a page full of numbers and a graph can be ten minutes of explanation.

Suppose, for example, that we wanted to explain the results of a compound rate of interest over a period of time. One way to do that would be to show you a page full of numbers such as Figure 6V. What if I could explain the results of a compound rate of interest, not by showing you a page full of numbers, but by taking you on a romantic adventure through life. Take a look at Figure 6W. That's the difference between a turn-off and a turn-on.

Another way of handling numbers is to organize them in such a way that they will not only prove your point, but invite audience participation and an element of surprise.

In Figure 6X, the audience is asked whether they would rather have their money in investment "A" or investment "B" for five years. Which would you choose? Most people chose investment "A," which, of course, is the wrong choice. For every $1,000 invested over five years, you would have ended up with $1,485 in investment "A," but $1,762

$1,000.
20% COMPOUND GROWTH RATE

YEAR	START OF YEAR	END OF YEAR	AVERAGE ANNUAL RETURN
1	$1,000 + 20% =	$1,200	20%
2	1,200 + 20% =	1,440	22%
3	1,440 + 20% =	1,728	24%
4	1,728 + 20% =	2,073	26%
5	2,073 + 20% =	2,488	29%
6	2,488 + 20% =	2,985	33%
7	2,985 + 20% =	3,583	36%
8	3,583 + 20% =	4,299	41%
9	4,299 + 20% =	5,159	46%
10	5,159 + 20% =	6,191	51.9%

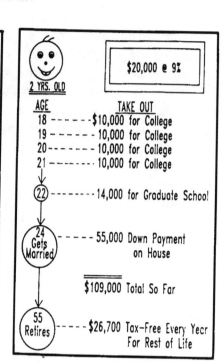

FIGURE 6V A page full of numbers. A textbook. A turn-off.

FIGURE 6W A journey through life. A romantic novel. A turn-on.

if you had put your money in investment "B." So if you use numbers, create a story to go with the numbers. Then remove all numbers that don't contribute to the story. If you do that you'll have it just right.

A final word about numbers. You can survive a misspelled word but not a mistake in arithmetic. When I am caught with a misspelled word, I smile and quote that famous American who said, "'Tis a shallow mind that can only think of one way to spell a word."

It's a different story with arithmetic. The mind concludes that if you are wrong about the money, you are probably wrong about other things, too. So triple check the addition and subtraction.

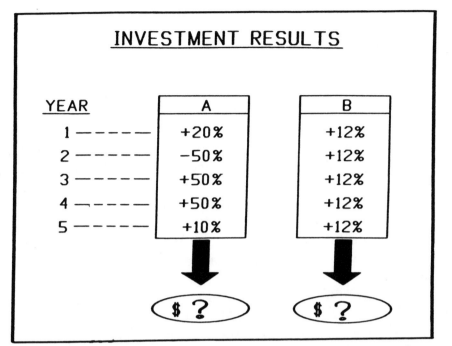

FIGURE 6X The organization of numbers can invite participation and cause surprise. The better choice is "B."

HUMAN INTEREST

A sure way to keep interest is to appeal to human interest. A good example is to tell the inside story. If you can start a sentence with, "The first thing I noticed about the Oval Office was . . . ," you've got them in the palm of your hand.

Not all of us have been in the Oval Office, but all of us have the inside story on something.

"What really happened on that day?"

"What is he or she really like?"

"How was the decision really made to buy X, do Y, or change to Z?"

People like things that are different, unusual, or a change of pace. The popularity of Trivial Pursuit is no accident. For example, in some of my presentations I use a rustic, crooked stick for a pointer. I have a trivial (but true) story that goes with the stick. It concerns:

Where I found it—Joyce Kilmer National Park.

What's different about that—largest stand of virgin timber in the eastern United States.

Who was Joyce Kilmer?—a writer and a poet.

Was Joyce Kilmer a man or a woman?—a man; he died in his early twenties on a battlefield in France in World War I.

He left us a poem of which every person in the room knows the first two lines: "I think that I shall never see/A poem as lovely as a—," and a beautiful national park of virgin timber in western North Carolina.

The curiosity of people in such things never ceases to amaze me. Often to save time, I leave out the story of the stick. Invariably, when I do, people come up after the presentation and ask me about the stick.

An interesting sidelight is that years later, people will have forgotten my name but they always remember me as the man with the stick.

The popular PBS TV program *Wall Street Week* has as its guest the heavy-hitters and deep-thinkers of the world of finance. But the most frequently asked question about the program concerns none of these big names. It concerns a woman who is seen only for a few seconds as she escorts the host onto the set. She never says anything. The most frequently asked question is, "Who is that woman?"

I'll never forget a presentation made by a colleague of mine. He was told that this would be an important meeting of important people and this should be a formal presentation. So at the appointed time he walks in dressed in (guess what?) a tux—complete with tails and a top hat. Well, let me tell you, no one in that meeting will ever forget that *formal* presentation.

Not many of us would feel comfortable pulling that off. But all of us can breathe life into our presentations by using human interest stories or trivia that are personal to us.

Another variation of human interest is the use of human interest *quesions*. Figure 6Y is a questionnaire concerning the abuse of credit. You can hear a pin drop when I show that questionnaire on the screen. I conceal the answer at the bottom using the revelation technique, and reveal it after a long pause when everyone has finished the questions.

People will pay attention and be interested when the subject directly pertains to them and their well-being. Human interest questions not only get attention, they are also a dramatic way of making your point.

THE FLASHING RED LIGHT EXAM

o DO YOU SPEND MORE THAN 20 PERCENT OF YOUR TAKE-HOME PAY ON MONTHLY INSTALLMENT BILLS, NOT INCLUDING MORTGAGE PAYMENTS?

o DO YOU REGULARLY RECEIVE "SECOND NOTICES."

o HAVE YOU RECENTLY BORROWED CASH WITH YOUR CREDIT CARD TO MEET HOUSEHOLD EXPENSES?

o DO YOU FIND IT IMPOSSIBLE TO PUT MONEY INTO A SAVINGS ACCOUNT?

o ARE YOU CURRENTLY BEING TELEPHONED BY A BILL COLLECTOR.

o DO YOU SECRETLY SUSPECT THAT YOUR CREDIT CARD SPENDING HAS GOTTEN OUT OF CONTROL?

o ARE YOU WORRIED ABOUT YOUR DEBTS?

o IS THERE FREQUENT STRESS AT HOME BECAUSE OF OVERDUE BILLS?

IF YOU ANSWERED "YES" MORE THAN ONCE, THEN THE RED LIGHT IS FLASHING FOR YOU.

FIGURE 6Y People will pay attention if the subject pertains to them and their well-being.

MAKE IT ALIVE, REAL, AND CURRENT

If you use references or quotes, consider a picture of the individual and a tidbit or two of human interest information.

For example, in talking about the profile of a millionaire, I introduced the subject by saying, "I want you to meet the richest man in America." (Show transparency picture.) "His name is Sam Walton. He owns the Wal-Mart Stores. He lives in Bentonville, Arkansas, population 9,920, drives a pick-up truck, and has breakfast at the Daylight Donut Shop."

Nobody ever went to sleep while being introduced to the richest man in America.

It's easy to make a transparency from a picture in a magazine or newspaper. First make a copy on the copier, then make the transparency from the copy. Works like a charm. Something else that will impress your audience is to show and use references or examples that are hot off the press, such as current articles from *The Wall Street Journal,* the local paper, or current magazines.

An attention-getting technique is to cut out the article and make a transparency out of it. How's that for showing how much you're on top of the subject? And it gives the audience the feeling that they are in-the-know with the latest scoop.

HOW TO STAY AWAKE DURING A FILM OR VIDEO

Even the best can lose an audience during a film or video.

How do we keep them awake during this traditional snooze time? More importantly, how do we insure that they get from the film the reason for showing it?

Here's how.

First, before showing the video, give the audience a preview of what it's about. Second, tell them what to watch for. Third, tell them what questions we will discuss when it's over.

Here's one of the cleverest things I have ever seen. A presenter in introducing a film suggested that the audience pay particular attention to the very last line, since that was the key to the entire film and would be the subject of discussion at the end of the film.

FIGURE 6Z Use articles and quotes that are hot off the press.

Well, have you ever tried to watch and listen for the last line in a film? Problem is, you never know when it's coming. Especially if you don't know how long the film is. Every line could be the last line.

HANDOUTS

Let's talk about handouts. Are they friend or foe? Should they be distributed at the beginning or at the end?

Handouts, if properly used, can greatly enhance audience attention and interest. On the other hand, if not properly used, they can more than detract—they can cause you to lose the audience.

Whether or not to have a handout depends on the subject, your objective, the complexity of the material, and the expected use of the information. But if in doubt, have a handout. You have nothing to lose and much to gain. So does your audience.

The most common approach to handouts is to simply reproduce all the visual aids and distribute them at the beginning of the presentation. If you do this you are almost sure to lose the audience. You have just created an environment for a heads-down audience. You have lost the effect of your strongest and most important visual aid—yourself. Worse still, the audience, instead of being *with* you, will tend to be a visual aid or two *ahead* of you.

What to do? What *not* to do is to distribute a complete copy of the handout in advance. Yet there can be certain material like a flow chart or a schematic diagram for which a handout would be helpful. It would allow the audience to make notes directly on the handout.

Here's a suggested way of handling that. Typically, in an hour's presentation, there would not be more than three or four handout sheets that would truly be helpful for note taking. Make separate copies of these and distribute them individually only when you come to that subject in the presentation. Additional handout material should be distributed at the end of the presentation. A convenient and painless way of handling this is to stack the handouts on a table near the door so your audience can pick up a copy on the way out.

Are there any exceptions to this? There sure are.

Suppose I distributed a complete set of handouts in advance, but when you looked at the handout and flipped through it, there was nothing on it. Every page looked something like Figure 6AA.

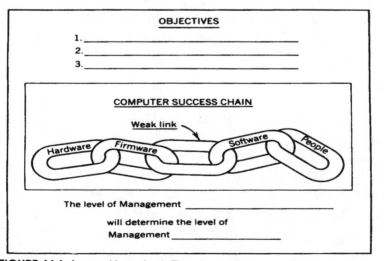

FIGURE 6AA A good handout. They hear, they see, they write it down.

The handout consisted of nothing but a bare-bones outline of a format with most of it blank. One look at this and the audience quickly understands that there is no point in looking ahead because there is nothing to see.

But now watch what happens. I project the first overhead on the screen. As I speak about the content I fill in the blanks by writing directly on the transparency with a felt-tip pen. And so, using key words, I complete the session objectives I write "management involvement" on the unnamed link of the chain, and I fill in the blanks for the statement at the bottom so it will read, "The level of Management *involvement* will determine the level of Management *satisfaction*."

What do you think the audience is doing with their copies of this handout as I am filling in the blanks? That's right. They are also filling in the blanks.

And so we have created the perfect environment for people to learn, understand, and retain. In the words of Confucius, they hear it, they see it, and they do it.

And here's a trick to create efficient and effective handouts. Double reduce your 8½ x 11 originals of the visuals on a copier. Then cut and paste them four to a page like Figure 6BB.

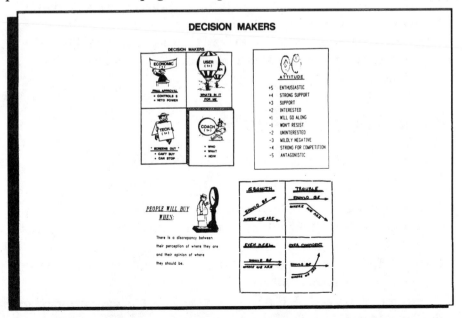

FIGURE 6BB Reduce visuals on a copier and paste four on a page for handout.

SEATING ARRANGEMENTS

Could the seating arrangements have anything to do with audience attention, interest, and participation?

You bet your sweet apples it could.

What is the worst way to set up a room? The worst way is the way most rooms are set up most of the time. Take a look at Figure 6CC for examples of good and bad. By the way, most room arrangements are determined by the janitorial staff.

From top to bottom: The U-shaped is the best of the bunch when you want group participation. It is far superior to the elongated conference table with unnecessary and unequal distance from the presenter, and very bad viewing for those toward the back of the table.

Next, the angled tables put two-thirds of the people closer to the presenter and allow them to see each other.

The third example shows the herringbone pattern which, again, allows the participants to see each other as opposed to the stereotyped classroom arrangement.

The final example shows an amphitheater or horseshoe seating arrangement as opposed to a military formation. Again, not as formal, more open, able to see others, and more conducive to participation.

Generally, wide and flat is better than narrow and deep. If there are windows in the room, arrange it so that it is the presenter who can look out the windows, not the audience. And don't have a clock in view of the audience.

CONVICTION AND ENTHUSIASM

Nothing great was ever achieved without enthusiasm.
- Ralph Waldo Emerson

We said earlier that a key part of our job is to persuade other people to a course of action we would like them to take. That being the case, lets talk about the greatest principle of persuasion that exists.

So powerful is it, that there is nothing that is a close second. With this ingredient you can forget all others.

Without it, you need all the help you can get. The magic ingredient is ENTHUSIASM.

ROOM ARRANGEMENTS

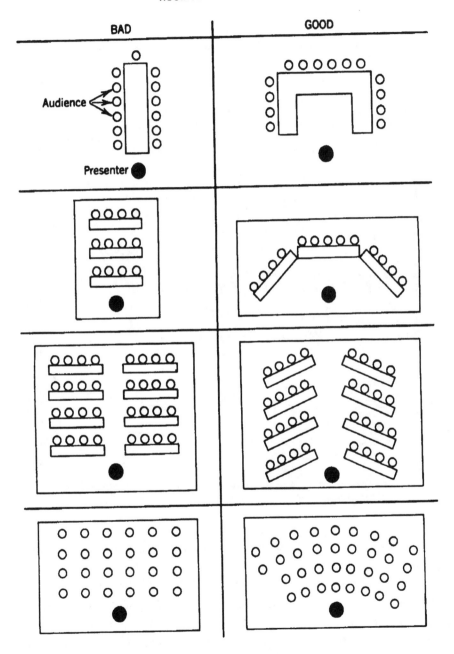

FIGURE 6CC The worst way to set up a room is the way most rooms are set up most of the time.

There is a simple truth in figure 6DD that I learned from people wiser than myself.

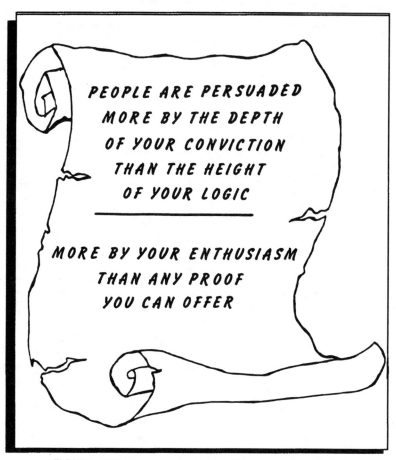

PEOPLE ARE PERSUADED
MORE BY THE DEPTH
OF YOUR CONVICTION
THAN THE HEIGHT
OF YOUR LOGIC

MORE BY YOUR ENTHUSIASM
THAN ANY PROOF
YOU CAN OFFER

FIGURE 6DD The greatest principle of persuasion.

If you believe you could use some help in the area of enthusiasm, let me share two thoughts.

First, you should ponder your own belief and depth of conviction in the subject. If you have doubts, reservations, or conditional allegiance to the subject, then you should not be making that presentation. So do some soul searching or find another subject to which you can make a total commitment.

Second, I ask you to think of the audience in this context. If you are making a one-hour presentation to 40 people, then you are taking up 40 hours of other people's time. If you are going to take up the equivalent of one week of your audience's time, then they deserve the very best you've got to give.

Or look at it this way. If you are giving a one-hour presentation to 40 people, and if their average annual salary is $60,000, then the collective value of that one hour is $1,200. Is what you have to say worth $20 a minute?

The thought of $20 a minute will get my juices flowing real good, real fast.

TALK IN THREES AND CONTRAST

Studies have been done of the great speakers throughout recorded history. Two common denominators stand out. The first is called a "three- part list," or we could simply say "speaking in threes." Here are some examples:

Of the people,

By the people,

For the people.

I came.

I saw.

I conquered.

Friends,

Romans,

Countrymen,

Lend me your ears.

A second characteristic of great speakers is their use of contrast. For example:

Ask not what your country can do for you.
Ask what you can do for your country.

Or how about a study in contrast from the surface of the moon:

That's one small step for man;
One giant leap for mankind.

Or what about the best known and most quoted verse in all of English literature:

To be
Or not to be.
That is the question.

If you are clever you can combine speaking in threes with contrast. The master of this was Winston Churchill. You may recall that he said:

Never in the field of human conflict has
So much
Been owed by so many
To so few.

Here we see a list of three, but notice that item number three is in contrast to the other two.

We can all be more effective if we speak in threes and in contrast. I'm practicing up on it myself. For example, the first thing I said in this book was:

We're not here to talk about

Hardware

Software

or Applications.

I followed this with another list of threes:

What we're here to talk about is:

Money

Fame

Glory

YOU ARE THE MESSAGE

The speech coach and debate coach for the last two presidents of the United States is Roger Ailes. He wrote a book with the title *You Are The Message*. By that he means that the best way to get what you want is to be who you are. Some people have the idea that they should go into an act or a role play when they stand up to talk. Roger Ailes says that is absolutely the wrong thing to do. If you fake it, if you act or role play, the audience will perceive that it's not naturally you. They will tune you out and turn you off.

There are three types of presenters, as shown in Figure 6EE. The blue, the green, and the red. The blue are the heavy thinkers. These are the brainy, analytical types. The red are the more emotional and charismatic types. In the middle are those who put on a mask and try to be something they are not. This is what Roger Ailes says we should never do.

When I show Figure 6EE to a live audience, I cover up the names at the bottom and ask the audience which they think would be the better speaker or presenter. The answer is always the same. They always say the red. I then reveal the names at the bottom. The names prove conclusively that whether you are blue or red, you can be good and you can be effective. So whether you're blue or red, go all the way. Be all blue or all red. Do not get stuck in the middle.

YOU ARE THE MESSAGE

BLUE	GREEN	RED
ANALYTICAL	CAUTIOUS	EMOTIONAL
DELIBERATE	TRADITIONAL	INSTINCTIVE
RESTRAINED	NEUTRAL	CHARISMATIC
INTELLECTUAL	BORING	IMPULSIVE

FIGURE 6EE Be all blue or all red. Do not get stuck in the middle.

If the plain-speaking Harry Truman had tried to sound like the sophisticated Winston Churchill, he would have been perceived to be a phony.

The names of the blue and the red dispel another myth. Some think style and substance are mutually exclusive, i.e., if you have style you must be a lightweight thinker. Or if you have substance you must be boring. The names of the real people in Figure 6EE are the only proof we need to put that myth to bed.

NONVERBAL COMMUNICATIONS

Here is an amazing finding. Of the total impact of your presentation, only 7% is determined by the words you use, 38% is determined by the tone of your voice, and 55% by your nonverbal communications.

FIGURE 6FF Actions speak louder than words.

So smile, move, look 'em in the eye, and gesture to show your conviction. If you say something one way verbally, but a different way nonverbally, your audience will always choose the nonverbal. It's far easier to lie verbally than it is nonverbally. If, for example, you stand up, look at the floor, and say, "I'm happy to be here," your nonverbal message says just the opposite. Or, if you put your hands on your hips, stand like the Sundance Kid, and say, "You all feel free to ask any question at any time," your body language says, "You better not ask any questions."

The man some say is the greatest comedian of all time never spoke a word. Charlie Chaplin did it all nonverbally. And the best performances of Red Skelton were 100% word free.

When professionals are judging a new television personality, they will watch him or her with the sound off, and ask themselves, "Do I see anything that makes me want to turn the sound up?" So do not hide behind a lectern and read words while trying to be polished, perfect, and detached. People want to listen to people who are warm, friendly, and human.

At the beginning of this chapter we said a shot of Hot Spice every six to eight minutes would help you keep the attention and interest of the audience. You may have been wondering what all this Hot Spice looks like or tastes like. Well, it can be stories, games, exercises, contests, exciting visuals, free gifts, or anything that involves one of the four things people find most interesting—sex, health, money, or themselves.

Remember, it is important that we tie in the Hot Spice to the subject. If you can do that it's a sure-fire way of making your point, having it understood and remembered. If you're interested in doing well and having the audience say, "That was a great presentation," then you need some Hot Spice. That's what will breathe life, humor, and excitement into your presentation. It will make the difference between plain vanilla and a banana split.

A good idea is to set yourself up a Hot Spice file. Then as you run across cartoons, jokes (that fit your chemistry), games, gimmicks, tricks, and so on, just drop them in your spice file. That makes it easy to pick and choose from an inventory and fit the spice to the presentation.

If your needs are immediate and you don't have an inventory of spice, just go to the magazine stand in the larger book stores. There in the general area of crossword puzzles you will find a magazine by the name of *Games*. It's Hot Spice from cover to cover.

Jokes and stories are examples of Hot Spice, but they need to fit your chemistry. In fact, you need to feel natural and comfortable with all the spice you use. For example, not everyone would feel comfortable doing the following:

- Crumpling up speech notes and throwing them on the floor (even though they're blank paper).
- Throwing a ball to someone in the audience.
- Doing a magic trick.
- Pouring water to overflow a glass.
- Setting off a firecracker.
- Guessing the number of jelly beans in a glass and relating the number to a point you're making.

Take a look at figure 6GG. "Let's see if we can identify famous people just by their hair styles."

FIGURE 6GG You don't have to know all the details to come to the right conclusion.

The answers are: Princess Di, Ronald Reagan, Captain Kangaroo, Albert Einstein, George Washington, Bo Derek, Elvis Presley, Farrah Fawcett, Groucho Marx, and William Shakespeare.

This can be used to illustrate that you don't have to know all the details to come to the right conclusion, or that some characteristics dominate all others.

If I wanted to talk about something important that was going to happen on Tuesday, I might introduce the subject with the piece of spice shown in Figure 6HH.

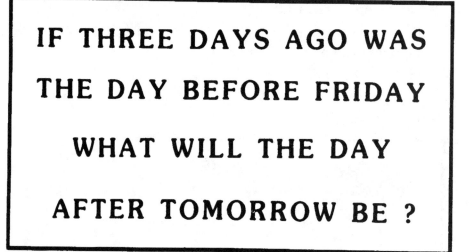

FIGURE 6HH Example of hot spice to focus attention on a specific day.

By changing the word *Friday* I can cause the right answer to be any day I want it to be.

Figure 6II never ceases to amaze me. Whenever I use it people start writing down those words.

You can use it to talk about the power of words. For example, when a large national retailer wanted to break into the plastic credit card business they chose one of these words as the name of their credit card.

Speaking of words, the most powerful word combinations in the English language are shown in Figure 6JJ.

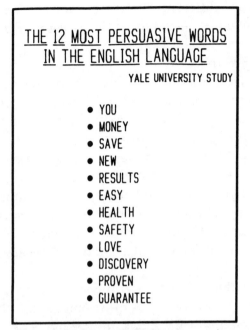

FIGURE 6II Powerful single words.

FIGURE 6JJ The most powerful word combinations in the English language.

Here's something different. If you are going to refer to an event or date in history, you can get copies of the *New York Times* on any date since 1851.

It's interesting to relate what else was going on in the world on a particular date that is important in your presentation.

A variation of this is to get newspapers made up with a fake headline that pertains to your subject, to this particular meeting, or to someone on the program or in the audience.

Any time I'm talking about money, I have a two-minute story of a millionaire. It's a secret that's 4,000 years old. It comes from the ancient city of Babylon. At the end of the story I recommend they take a trip to their local public library to check out the book *The Richest Man in Babylon* by George S. Clason. And there in a story just twelve pages long, they will learn the secret that is today 4,000 years old. They sure write that down.

In my presentation I build in audience participation by asking questions. I then give away prizes to whomever has the first correct answer. The prizes are my first book, my second book, my videotape, or my audiotape. I give them a choice. A by-product of this is that it promotes my books and tapes, and increases the sales of these products at the end of the presentation.

A change-of-pace peak that works for me is to play "two truths and a lie." Members of the audience are invited on a voluntary basis to tell three pieces of information about themselves—two of which are true, and one of which is a lie. The audience is asked to guess which one is the lie. The winner who stumps the audience gets a prize.

Another winning piece of Hot Spice is an audience-participation exercise. Figure 6KK is an example of my pop quiz.

As you think about it you will come up with your own Hot Spice that's perfect for your chemistry and your personality.

HOW WELL DO I KNOW MY CUSTOMER

1. My customer's biggest competitor is _____.

2. The single greatest strength of that competitor is
_____.

3. The most common complaint or objection to my customer's
product or service is _____.

4. Pending legislation would affect my customer as follows:
_____.

5. The single biggest problem in my customer's industry is:
_____.

6. The president's highest priority goal or objective is:
_____.

7. The five year trend of my customer's marketshare has been
_____.

8. My customer's strategy is:
   a. Be low cost   b. Product differentiation   c. Niche player

9. The three greatest strengths of my customer's product or
service are:
   a. _____
   b. _____
   c. _____

10. My customer's largest customer is _____.

FIGURE 6KK Participation exercises get attention and keep interest.

VS.

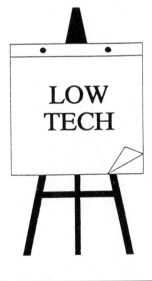

In putting our act together, what visual aid media should we use? Today's offerings range from the low-tech old reliables to the high-tech laser light shows. What's best for me? For my audience? For my purpose?

Before we get into that, let's review the benefits of using visual aids.

- Your audience is 43% more likely to be persuaded.
- Your audience will be willing to pay 26% more money for the same product or service.
- You can cover the same material in 25-40% less time.
- Learning is improved up to 200%
- Retention is improved up to 38%
- The presenter is perceived as being

  more professional

  more persuasive

  more credible

  more interesting

  and better prepared.

The worst visual aid is *no* visual aid. But what's best? And, more importantly, what's best for you?

Let's start with the visual aid with the fewest moving parts—the lowly flip chart—and move up the technology scale. Our objective is to sort through the glamour, the razzle-dazzle, the blinking lights, and come to some common sense conclusions you can use to choose what's best for you.

LET'S TALK ABOUT FLIP CHARTS

While high tech is marching on, the lowly flip chart continues to be one of the most effective presentation media of all, both as a mainstream presentation and as an alternate medium to change the pace and add spice. It's also the most economical. You can invest a lot of money in high tech, but don't presume it will be more effective than simple flip charts. The best visuals are usually the simplest. They should enhance your presentation, not upstage it.

There is more good news about flip charts. They can't break down, they don't require electrical outlets or extension cords, and there are no bulbs to burn out. There is hardly anything that can go wrong with a flip-chart presentation. It may be low tech, but it's high reliability.

And guess where your cheat sheet is? That's right, it's on the flip charts themselves, written lightly in pencil so the audience can't see.

On the other hand, flip charts are not practical if the group size is larger than 50 at tables, or 100 seated theater-style. They also tend to get dog-eared and tattered with use, and are somewhat awkward to travel with.

THE POSTER MACHINE (High Tech Flip Charts)

Here is a high-tech gadget with low-tech ease-of-use. Take any 8½ x 11 piece of paper, insert it into the poster machine like you would in a copy machine, press the button and ten seconds later out comes a flip-chart-sized copy in color. The content can be graphics or cartoons, printed bullets, or any combination of elements. So you can be as fancy as you like producing a page on your PC (personal computer). Then convert it to a flip-chart-sized page. If you don't want to buy a poster machine, you may find a distributor who will let you use one on a per-page charge basis. Check the yellow pages under "Audio-Visual."

Just so you'll know, there are also on-line plotters specifically designed for flip-chart-sized paper. But this is big money for the big time where there's heavy need and frequent use.

DESKTOP FLIP CHARTS

I am often asked what I think of using desktop flip charts. My opinion is that you'll get less than half the results if you go halfway. To get the biggest bang with little additional effort, go all the way and give your client or customer a stand-up, 100% professional presentation.

One of our objectives is to differentiate ourselves from our competition. If your competitor gives any kind of presentation, it's a good bet it's desktop flips. Don't do what the enemy does. Do something different and better.

AN EXAMPLE OF THE BEST

One of the best marketing tools I ever saw was not a sales pitch, but an educational seminar on computer concepts for seven days. Is that a misprint? No, I said seven days—and at a remote location. Well, I guess that's fine to train programmers. But wait, this is not for programmers. The only people allowed to attend are presidents and chairmen of the board.

There are no prepared visual aids of any kind. The only props for seven days are two flip-chart stands with blank paper and magic markers. The presenter creates his visuals as he talks by writing and drawing on the flip charts in realtime. Although this gives the appearance of spontaneity, believe me, seven days of material has been carefully dissected, organized, and planned for each blank page. Exact words that will go on every page are planned, their position on the chart is planned, and the color is planned. Multicolors are used for emphasis. Heavy use is made of graphics and pictorial representations, and the drawing is carefully rehearsed. Nothing is left to chance, including *which* flip chart is used, *when* it is used, and *what* is left to viewing on *stand one* as the presenter moves to *stand number two*. Corners on strategic flip chart pages are turned down so the presenter can refer back to them at a future, predetermined time.

This requires a true professional who can write and talk at the same time, and has the timing and presence to control the audience. This style is more a controlled group discussion than it is a presentation. The blank flip charts, and writing or drawing in real time, not only give the presentation spontaneity but create an illusion for the audience that the presentation is being created just for them. In fact, at planned points in the presentation, the material is covered in such a way that an obvious question is not addressed. That question is always asked by someone in the audience. And the presenter—while giving the appearance of answering a question of interest to the audience—is merely continuing the planned sequence of the presentation.

PUTTING THE FLIP CHART TOGETHER

"But wait," you say. "There's just one big problem with flip charts. *I'm not an artist.*" You don't have to be. Listen up.

Let's say you want to use pictures, drawings, or cartoons. First we need to find copies of originals we want to use. Don't worry about the physical size. We'll take care of that in a minute. Let me suggest four sources. The first is the *Yellow Pages.* Just look up the subject matter under the appropriate heading and five will get you ten that you'll find a picture of what you want.

The second source is children's coloring books.

The third source is clip art. These are booklets of nothing but pictures, symbols, and cartoons. You can pick them up at an art supply store, or some office supply stores. Just ask for *clip art.* They will know what you're talking about.

Finally, if you have access to a PC, there's a bundle of graphic and clip art available from numerous software packages.

The next step is to transfer the pictures, symbols, and cartoons we have selected to flip charts. The process is simple. First we make a transparency of the item. Then we place it on a projector and project it on to a blank flip-chart page. By moving the projector closer or further away we can get any size we want. Using a pencil, we now trace the projected image on to the flip-chart paper. The final step is to trace over our pencil marks with Magic Markers.

How about lettering? You will be surprised at how well you can do yourself with just a little practice and patience. A couple of tips will be helpful.

Use an $8^{1}/_{2}$ x 11 piece of graph paper to plan the layout, establish the horizontal and vertical center lines, and position the lettering and the drawing in rough form. If you're into this in a big way, you can get a form from the supplier of flip-chart paper that does the same thing. It's called a flip-chart planning sheet.

Then select the flip-chart paper that has light blue lines on it for horizontal and vertical alignment. If you turn the paper over you can still see enough of the lines for printing alignment but they will not be visible to the audience.

A good rule of thumb is: No more than six lines, and no more than eight to ten words per page. Be sure to make them big enough for the audience. Letters that are one inch tall can only be seen easily from less than 15 feet away. Letters that are two inches tall can be seen from 30 feet. Better to have them too big than too small. By the way, the light blue squares on the flip-chart paper are one inch in size.

Speaking of lettering, it's nice to have dots to the left of the bullets to set them off under the main heading. The problem comes in making them the same size with a Magic Marker. The first one looks just fine. But as you make the second one it becomes lopsided. In the process of correcting this it suddenly becomes bigger than the first one, and on and on goes the story. The simple solution is to buy stick-on dots. You can get them at an office supply store. They come in different colors and sizes.

If after giving freehand lettering a shot you decide it's not for you, there are some back-up solutions. You can find talent at the local trade school or art school. You will find many students eager for some part-time work—especially art school students. And don't be surprised to learn that the teenage daughter of your next-door neighbor is a whiz-bang with a Magic Marker and a flip chart.

You know, of course, that we need to staple a blank sheet to each completed flip-chart page. If you don't, the contents of the page behind it will show through—just enough to be a distraction to the audience. If you don't staple the blank page, I promise you will forget there is a blank page and end up turning two pages for every one—and that's a distraction.

Here is something that will happen to you every time. You are almost through the presentation when someone says, "Can you turn back to X; I have a question about X." Now comes the problem of going backward through the charts trying to find "X." You will always miss it the first time through and end up turning all the charts back over, going through them at least one more time, and maybe more. I don't know how long that takes, but it always seems to me like an eternity.

You can head this problem off at the pass by placing index tabs up and down the vertical side of the chart. Just cut out little pieces of a manila folder and Scotch tape them—get this—not to the page you want to turn to, but to the page in *front* of it. That way when you turn over the page with the tab, you have the right page showing.

You don't need a tab for every page, just those key pages you would expect to be asked about. This also makes an effective technique in a presentation if *you* want to refer back to a previous point you have established.

Before we leave the making of flip charts, just a couple of final points. Don't try to create a finished product the first time. You will find that it's off center, not vertically aligned, and so forth. Don't worry about it. This will be our rough draft chart. Just put a new page over it and redraw and reletter. It's easy to center and line things up by just moving the position of the top page. You will also notice an improvement in quality the second time around.

The chart maker's equivalent of hitting your finger with a hammer is misspelling a word on the last line of a chart. For some strange reason, it never happens at the top of the chart, always at the very bottom. Here's the solution. Lay the page on a pad of blank paper. Take a pen knife and cut out a small square or rectangle to remove the bad letter. If you press hard, you will also cut off a blank square or rectangle of exactly the same size in the blank page underneath. Having removed the square with the old letter, turn the page over and Scotch tape the blank square in the same spot from behind. It will fit exactly, of course, and even in the front row, they won't be able to see the repair work. You can now remake the correct letter on the new square.

To add pizzazz, interest, and attention to your presentation, you can create *overlays*. You do this by starting backward. That is, you create the final flip chart that has the total picture and details first. Then in front of it you simply have blank pages from which you have cut out sections to expose parts of the completed chart underneath. Using multiple cutout pages, you can sequentially reveal more and more of the completed chart. You can also color code each step of the revelation.

Another gimmick is to Scotch tape a second page to the bottom of a flip-chart page. This gives you a double-length page. You now have an expanded area to depict a roadmap-type concept, a flow of goods, or sequential steps. You can place the total picture before the audience. After the double-length flip-chart page is completed, you can cut just a couple of inches off the bottom of the second page. You can then fold it up and lightly tape it with masking tape. To solve the problem of tearing part of the paper off with the tape when you want to unfold it, do the following: Stick a small piece of masking tape permanently to the spot on the first page onto which you will be sticking the tape on the second page. That way you will be sticking masking tape on top of masking tape—and it works just fine. In fact, you can have multiple positions of tape down the page. This would allow you to reveal and talk about specific points while revealing them one point at a time. This can be very effective, but it's for small groups only, since a large group would not be able to see the bottom of the second page.

Another idea is to have actual cutouts of pie charts that you can hold in your hand to talk about, and then tape to a flip chart page that was designed for it.

In summary, if you take some blank pages, Magic Markers, patience, practice and time, then stir well, you will end up with a feast fit for any audience.

A flip chart is a workhorse that has been around forever. A flip-chart stand is standard equipment in most conference rooms and all hotel meeting rooms.

Flip charts are effective for small groups.

They allow the lights to be fully bright—facilitating interactive communications and good eye contact.

They are relatively easy to make.

They create an atmosphere of informality and promote audience participation.

They are easy to change, add to, and in general keep current.

They are economical.

They make it easy to have multiple colors.

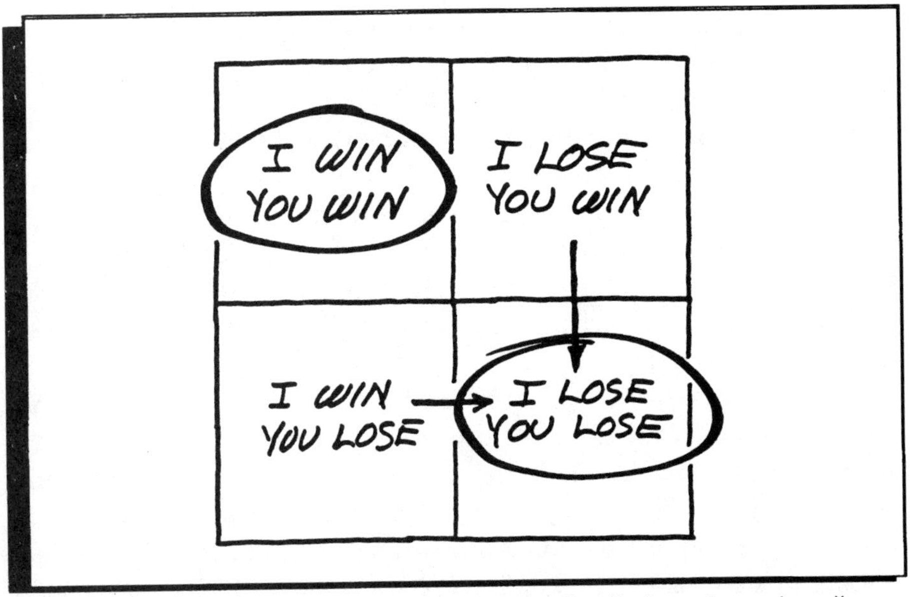

FIGURE 7A Drawing as you present creates the illusion of spontaneity.

They can create the illusion of spontaneity by drawing or writing in real time as you present.

OVERHEAD TRANSPARENCIES (FOILS)

Here it is: the all-time winner of the popularity contest—and for good reason. If you were to list all the functional capabilities you would like to have in a visual aid medium, then ask the question, "Which one will be the most effective with the least effort at the most reasonable cost?", the hands-down winner is overhead transparencies.

The world of high tech allows you to be as sophisticated or as simple as you would like to be. You can have everything from multicolor, multifoil overlays graphically created by a computer with an on-line plotter and transmitted to you over phone lines from a remote location, down to simple but colorful transparencies made in three seconds on your own copier.

If you are going to play in the transparency ball game, let me save you a lot of time and trouble. Don't stumble and fumble and make the same mistakes others have made.

What you should do is invest a couple hours of your time and learn from the experts at no cost to you. In every major city one or more suppliers will offer a no-charge graphics or transparency workshop. This will save you lots of time and trouble. The tricks of the trade are a skill that is best learned in a workshop and not out of a textbook. Further, the state of the art is advancing rapidly. A workshop is the best way to get up-to-date.

To find a workshop in your city, call 1-800-328-1371 or, turn to the *Yellow Pages* and look under "Audio-Visual." Check the ads. You may find a workshop mentioned in the ads. If not, call the companies with the larger ads and ask if they offer a workshop or training sessions on making transparencies. The ones that do are typically the suppliers that also offer the greatest variety of transparency material. That's what you are looking for—one-stop shopping for all your transparency supplies. In the workshop, you will get a working knowledge of how to make transparencies, how to use color, how to work with graphs, charts, and statistics. You will also learn the latest techniques and materials.

Creating a transparency presentation can be a low-budget operation. The vast majority of overhead transparencies are made by the user on his or her own copier or desktop foil maker. Transparency material is manufactured to work in the place of paper in most copiers. The folks that run the workshops can fix you up with the right material for your copier.

With such a variety of beautiful colors available, there is no excuse for using black and white. Some suppliers even supply an assortment of colors within the same box. You can produce transparencies with black on colored background, colors on clear background, clear letters on colored background, and colored letters on different colored backgrounds. Some are designed to fit in a copier. The more exotic ones require a desktop transparency maker.

Frames for Transparencies

This is a good news, bad news subject. The good news is that frames block out the light around the edge of a standard-size transparency and they are convenient for writing cheat notes to yourself. The bad news is that they are bulky and an odd size that does not fit well in most containers. They do not pack well for travel.

There is a new type of frame that overcomes the bad news and has an added advantage. It's called a flip frame. It's like a reusable transparent envelope inside which your transparency fits. It therefore provides protection against fingerprints, lint, and so on. It has flip panels on both sides that fold open when in use to provide the function of a frame and provide cheat sheet space. With the panels folded, punched holes along one edge permit convenient filing in a three-ring binder. If there is a disadvantage it's that you have to remember to flip open the panels and that you can't read your cheat sheet until the panels are open. Further, many presenters like to be able to look ahead and glance at their next cheat sheet. With the panels folded you can't do that. Without frames, you can stack your cheat sheet directly under its transparency. Then you can glance ahead and read the cheat notes through the next transparency.

The Computer Transparencies

The single best method of creating transparencies is a personal computer with a quality printer. So if you already have a PC, you're almost home. If you don't have a PC, do you have access to one through a friend, a business, a brother-in-law, or other source?

Next, we need a software package for graphics, symbols, and lettering. If you don't already have one, you should stop by a PC store. You will find you can do lettering in different styles, in different sizes, and position it where you want it. In addition, there are inventories of graphic formats, pictures, symbols, and drawings with flexibility of size and position.

Of course you have to pay a piece of change for the software, but it's well worth it if you are going to be putting together a number of presentations over a period of time. On the other hand, if this is a one-shot deal, there are other alternatives, including the most painless of all, coming next.

Farming It Out

If all of this sounds confusing and too much like work, have I got a deal for you.

Let the other guy do it for you. In fact, before the sun goes down you can have a done deal. It'll be professionally done and in living color. The cost is not as great as you might think. So get on the phone. Let your fingers do the walking under the heading of Audio-Visual.

But you don't get off scot-free. You have to do the basic design. What pictures? What words? Where? How big? The good news is that this can be in very rough form on a yellow pad. Just so the other guy can clearly understand what you want. He is a technician executing his skill, not a mind reader. So leave nothing to the imagination. If you spell it wrong, you get it back wrong—in living color.

In summary, overhead transparencies are:

Suitable for one-on-one or for an audience of up to 300

Relatively easy to create

Professional looking (if done right)

Convenient for travel

Effective with the room lights reasonably bright

Ideal if you need skip material to conserve time (unlike slides)

Informal, and promote audience participation

Not expensive if you have access to a personal computer with a quality printer and graphics software

Easy to maintain and keep current

Convenient for seeing what's on the screen (by looking down at the projector) without turning your back to the audience

Easy to use, and the projectors are easy to operate

Convenient for making handouts using the masters

Ideal for having a "cheat sheet" with each visual

In common use, and the projection equipment is readily available

Adaptable for using overlays and the "revelation technique"

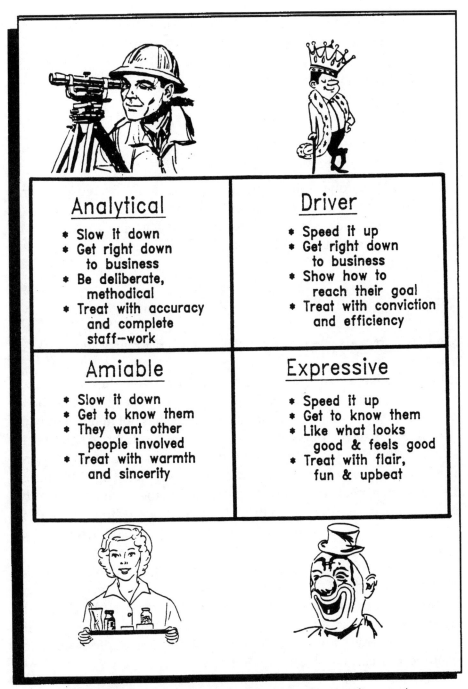

Analytical

* Slow it down
* Get right down
  to business
* Be deliberate,
  methodical
* Treat with accuracy
  and complete
  staff—work

Driver

* Speed it up
* Get right down
  to business
* Show how to
  reach their goal
* Treat with conviction
  and efficiency

Amiable

* Slow it down
* Get to know them
* They want other
  people involved
* Treat with warmth
  and sincerity

Expressive

* Speed it up
* Get to know them
* Like what looks
  good & feels good
* Treat with flair,
  fun & upbeat

FIGURE 7B Transparencies are ideal for using overlays and
the "revelation technique."

(covering part of a transparency to shield it from the projector light, thus controlling what is revealed and when)

On the other hand, transparencies:

Are not practical for an audience of more than 300 people

Collect lint and fingerprints if unprotected

Can tend to turn yellow with age

Cause a "keystone" effect with a large screen (the image is wider at the top of the screen than at the bottom). Note: This can be solved by screens that tilt forward, or by correcting the distortion by using masking tape on the projector top.

SLIDES

Not long ago, slides were only for those with big bucks and weeks of patience!

But times have changed. As high tech marches on, the cost of slides has fallen dramatically. The wait time is now days or hours, instead of weeks. The key is shopping around. High tech has not fallen evenly on everyone. Some still follow the old ways with the old price and the old wait. On the other hand, there are those who can generate words and music on their color PC screen, and give you a handful of slides before the first coffee break. In no other area of this business are price, quality, and service comparison more important. So do your homework. You won't get home free. But you will get home without paying the price of a limousine.

The major advantage of slides is that for a large audience (over 300) it's the only medium they can clearly see other than film.

Slides look professional. They are excellent if your objective is to inform or entertain. They are very portable. And they are the only practical medium for presentations that require photographs, for example, a presentation on how to dress for success.

If, however, your objective is to persuade other people to a course of action you would like them to take, then slides have a downside.

- They are perceived as formal and impersonal.
- They require the lights to be down.
- They can be expensive.
- They can be awkward, if not difficult, to make changes to and keep current.
- The presenter does not have the same degree of control over the presentation that he does with flip charts or transparencies.

There is another aspect to slides that is difficult to put into words. Let me see if I can explain it this way.

One of the big events in IBM is the annual kick-off meeting in January held at all branch offices throughout the country. For this occasion, material is sent to the branches from Headquarters about new products, new services, new marketing programs, and so on. But for the sales force, the biggest announcement of all is the Sales Compensation Plan or simply the Sales Plan, as it is called in the bull pen.

If a sales plan is announced with technicolor slides and a Headquarters script, it is received with skepticism, doubt, and the certainty that it must not be any good or else they would not have gone to so much trouble and expense to try to convince the sales force how great-it's-gonna-be. If it was really any good you wouldn't need pictures in living color to convince 'em.

MOVIES

This is the big time. This is the main tent show to the multitudes. This is the businessperson's answer to Hollywood. Color this money. If you're into movies then you already have staff experts on the subject, or you have the big bucks to pay the price for the professionals this medium demands. So let's move on to another subject that is more "real world" to most of us.

VIDEO

Coming on strong and growing in use every day is video. More and more conference rooms, meeting rooms, training rooms, and convention facilities are being equipped for video. Using professionally created tapes, video can combine the excitement of the movies with the interactive discussion of flip charts or overheads.

The library of tapes is growing rapidly. So whatever your subject of interest, there's a good chance you can buy or rent a tape on it for a lot less money and trouble than it would take to develop it yourself in any medium. Whether you want to improve your golf swing or learn negotiating skills, there is a tape for you.

The key to effective use of video is how you manipulate it. The way not to use it is to press the start button and let it run for an hour, expecting the machine to do your work for you. The right way is to use it to play a series of interrupted vignettes where you stop and discuss the content, key points, and conclusions along the way. The presenter becomes a facilitator, directing a discussion and coming to conclusions, using video as a medium for setting the stage and stimulating the discussion.

It can be extremely effective (when properly used) for training—especially if integrated with case studies and role plays. And video is not limited to a TV screen. There is equipment that will project it onto a big screen, and it's getting better all the time.

MISCELLANEOUS AND OTHER

We have purposely left out of this discussion blackboards, white boards, flannel boards, magnetics, etc. Outside of a classroom environment they have little use in presentations, so let's move on up the high-tech scale.

THE COMPUTER

I am the luckiest guy in the world. Over 30 years ago by blind luck I went to work for a computer company. I was there when the computer was born. I have lived with the computer baby as it grew through childhood and adolescence into adulthood. How exciting has been the journey. How dramatic have been the changes and the effect on our daily lives. Who would ever have thought that I would have on my desk a computer 20 times more powerful than the first one I sold which took up the entire basement of an office building.

Today, the PC is your best tool for designing slides or transparencies. If you don't have a color plotter you can transmit the finished design to a service that has one and will do it for you with immediate turnaround. You will learn other techniques at the half-day visual aid workshop we have talked about.

But there are even more exciting uses of the computer in giving and supporting presentations.

LIVE COMPUTER PRESENTATIONS

We have been talking about using the computer off-line to produce slides or transparencies. Now let's go to the edge of space and use the computer to give a live on-line presentation. Software packages are now available that let you produce and direct your own show in color and in motion. We can even project the show onto a large screen by placing a display projection panel (like a one-foot-square window) on an overhead projector. The display panel is plugged into the computer. The images from the computer are transferred to the display panel, and then projected onto a screen just as though they were transparencies laying on top of the projector. The lights need to be dimmed, but the projected image is getting brighter and clearer as technology continues its march to who-knows-where.

The next step (and it's here today) is called Multimedia. This is a combination of new hardware technology and new software that blends together—listen to this—video, sound, animation, and images with text and graphics in an exciting and interactive package. And all that on a desktop computer. What more could a presenter want?

ON-LINE AUDIENCE RESPONSE

There's more. Each member of your audience can have a ten-key pad that's on-line to your PC at the front of the room. As opinions are asked and questions raised, the audience enters their individual response on their ten-key pad, and the collective results are displayed live and graphically from the computer to a large screen.

What creative opportunities this offers for teaching, training, and presentation! We have said many times that the greatest visual aid of all is you. But now the star of the show can be the audience themselves. Thus we can add an entirely new dimension to our communication thinking. We are, however, burdened with our old paradigms, and have yet to grasp the potential of computerized group dynamics. We need new creative thinking in conceptual approaches, design, and structure.

Is this the wave of the future? Is it destined for mass acceptance and common use like the VCR? Or will it go the way of the CB radio? We shall see.

SO WHAT'S THE ANSWER—HIGH TECH OR LOW TECH?

The answer is—*you are the message*—you are the prime medium. How you behave, act, and speak is the most important part of the presentation. You are also the most versatile medium. Your power to project as a human being, to interact warmly and intelligently with the audience, and to modify the program on-the-fly as needed cannot be duplicated by any kind of electronics or laser holography. The audience may forget every word you say and every picture you show, but they will remember the image they have of you.

The bigger the electronic extravaganza, the smaller the presenter becomes. When the razzle-dazzle is over, someone has to stand up and ask the audience to do something, believe something, understand something, or buy something. If that someone is you, please realize that the electronic sound and light show has set the level of performance expectations of the audience. So if you are a mere mortal, and if your performance capabilities are something short of a laser show, then you will be conspicuous by contrast. Not exactly the kind of comparison one would like. You may be viewed as an usher in your own theater. Visual aids can play a strong role in supporting and enhancing the quality of a presentation, but they are not a substitute for the presenter.

The more complex the medium and the electronics, the greater is the requirement for professional and technical skills. Rare indeed is the person who is a high-tech audiovisual expert, a computer technician, and an excellent presenter. If you don't have all of those skills then you would need an experienced staff of experts backing you every step of the way. When things go wrong (and they will) you need a back-up, a by-pass, or a quick fix. If you don't, you may find yourself standing in a spotlight waiting in dead silence for the multimedia showstopper that never starts.

Furthermore, it's possible to look too polished, too slick. The medium can get in the way of the message. The credibility of you as a human being can decline as your reliance on high tech goes up. If you're reading from a teleprompter, it's hard to convince the audience of your conviction and commitment when they're wondering who wrote the script.

Conversely, the better the presenter the less the need or value of high tech. Further, if you're a little clumsy using a simple overhead projector, you'll really be up the creek if you try to run a console that looks like the flight deck of a 747.

SO WHAT SHOULD I DO?

Here are six things you can do in selecting and using visual aids that will put you a light year ahead of the pack.

1. *Make a decision and a commitment to use visual aids in your presentations.* The added value, the increased effectiveness and the greater probability of accomplishing your objective make it not only worthwhile, but an opportunity too good to miss.

2. *Simplify, Simplify, Simplify.* We lose effectiveness and we confuse our customers and our clients with the complexity and the technicalities of the subject. A good visual aid looks like a billboard on an interstate highway that people could read going by at 65 MPH.

3. *Use Color.* Here's why:

- It's 50 to 85% more effective in selling products and ideas.
- It accelerates learning, retention, and recall by 55 to 78%.
- It improves and increases comprehension up to 73%.

4. *Use graphs, charts, pictures and cartoons.* People will comprehend the main point of a simple graph or chart in about five seconds. They may never get the main point from a page full of numbers—let alone remember it. And a screen full of words is like hearing through the eyes. One picture is worth eight minutes of words.

5. *Select your visual aid medium based on your comfort and your confidence in its use.* A good presentation depends on how well you use the weapons you choose—not where they fit on the scale of technology. You're more likely to hit the bull's eye with a dart than a laser gun if you can't find the on/off switch. And more importantly (one more time), the greatest visual aid of all is you. The gadgets are not even a close second.

6. *Rehearse, Rehearse, Rehearse.* There is nothing else you can do that will give you a bigger bang for less effort. Do not do what the pros would never try—perform without practice.

The Presenter's Secret Weapon

(The Question)

What would you guess is the single most important weapon to use in getting attention, keeping interest, and receiving feedback on how you're doing?

You just read the correct answer. It's the question.

Nothing can do so much for so many as the question. And nothing is as effective as the question to give you immediate feedback on the comprehension, understanding, and agreement of the audience. Questions are an essential and integral part of an effective presentation. Not just any question, but well-thought-out, planned, and prepositioned questions. And the planned question is an important item on your cheat sheet.

You should consider a question for either the introduction of a key point or as a way of finalizing the key point, or both.

For example, in presenting my company's corporate strategy, I introduce a key point by asking the audience whether they think our company is primarily a technology-driven company or primarily a market-driven company. Well, let me tell you, that really gets the juices flowing. Most people had never thought about the company in those terms. Not only do they voluntarily start responding, they start arguing with each other. Nobody ever went to sleep during that question, or the presentation of the material that followed on that subject.

The key to the question is to make it stimulating and thought-provoking: questions that call on experience, views, or opinions. Questions that start with phrases like, "What is your opinion of . . . ?" or, "What is the first thing you would do if . . . ?" or, "What do you think is the cause of . . . ?"

What we do *not* want are mundane questions with a self-evident answer of yes or no.

You do want to cause early success with the audience, so you'll want the first few questions to be easy to answer.

The most dramatic and tongue-in-cheek example of causing early success I ever saw was a presenter who asked a member of the audience to pick a number between one and ten. He responded with "four." The presenter said, "That's the correct answer." Of course, any answer would have been the correct answer.

On a more serious note, you should ask questions that:

- Relate to the key point you are presenting
- Are clear and concise
- Emphasize one point only
- Reveal the audience's understanding

There are different types of questions and different questioning techniques. Here are some types of questions that are suited for an audience size of fewer than 50 people.

THE RIFLE SHOT QUESTION

This is where you make eye contact with a specific individual, call him by name, then ask the question. This is the most common type of question.

THE TIME BOMB QUESTION

This is where you ask the question of the audience as a group, then call on a specific person to answer only after you have finished the question. This is an effective technique for getting attention and keeping interest. After a few of these types of questions, the audience will really perk up since they don't know who is going to be called on to answer—and nobody wants to be embarrassed by not knowing what the question was.

THE RICOCHET QUESTION

This is where you redirect a question that has been asked of you to another member of the audience. This is a good technique if you want a little more time to think about your answer. It is also helpful in assessing the understanding of the audience about the subject. It's effective for audience participation and especially good for handling some types of troublemakers, as we shall see in Chapter 9.

THE REBOUND QUESTION

This is where the presenter rephrases the question and directs it back to the person who asked it. This technique is also good for certain types of troublemakers and tends to reduce or eliminate frivolous questions.

Which type of question is the best?

No single one, but *all* of the above. It is best to have a mix of questions, with the inherent elements of suspense and surprise.

These types of questioning techniques presuppose that you either know the people or they have tent cards to facilitate calling them by name. But what if you don't know the people, and they don't have tent cards? The answer is a seating chart. A seating chart is an $8^1/2 \times 11$ piece of paper with the names of the people and their relative position in the room.

The simplest and easiest way to get a seating chart is to ask the host or person running the meeting if they have one. Sometimes, but not often, they will.

The next best way is to sit in on the meeting kick-off if the attendees are asked to introduce themselves. Have the room arrangement

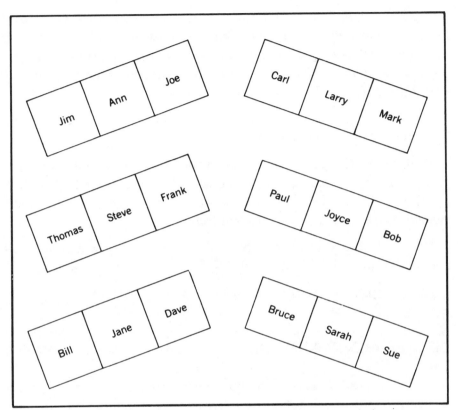

FIGURE 8A A seating chart will allow us to call on people by name.

roughed out with the boxes for each position. Then all you have to do is write their names in the boxes. This has the added advantage that you can also make brief notes about special backgrounds, experiences, skills, and so forth. This will allow you to personalize and tailor your questions to specific individuals.

Another way of getting a seating chart with names is to sit in the back of the room and ask a staff member, or another presenter who is familiar with the audience, to help you fill in the names.

If none of the above works you can still sit in on other presentations and listen to names as they are used by other presenters, or by attendees among themselves before the meeting and at coffee breaks. Using this technique, you can get at least 25% of the names. That's all you need to personalize your questions.

In any event, get some names. You want to direct your question to John by name, not by, "Hey you."

Well, all that Q & A is fine for a small audience, but what if it's a larger group? You can't really have questions and answers for a large group, right? Wrong. You sure can have questions for a large group—you just change your style and use a different technique.

The key is to phrase the question in such a way that it causes a short answer and provides a hint to the type of answer we are looking for.

For example, we have the sing-a-long.

THE SING-ALONG QUESTION

Here the question is directed not to an individual, but to the entire audience. Examples: "The bottom line reason we're in business is to make _____" (What?). Or, if I were talking about the relationship between unit cost and volume, I might say, "If I increase the volume the unit cost will go _____" (Which way?).

Another version of the sing-along question is to ask for a show of hands on a subject, an opinion, an experience, and so on.

THE MULTIPLE CHOICE QUESTION

Here we give the audience a hint by suggesting some answers. For example, in talking about lawyers I make the following statement: "You would probably guess that we have more lawyers per 1000 of population than the Japanese. . . . But how many more? . . . Twice as many? . . . Three times as many? . . . Ten times as many?" The key to this technique is to make brief eye contact with multiple people as you call out the multiple choices. At the same time extend your arm in a gesture of directing the question to multiple people.

THE ASK AND ANSWER QUESTION

This is a technique where you ask a question, pause, and then answer it yourself. For example, "Of all the stockbrokers in the country, what percent would you guess don't own any stock?" (Pause) "Would you believe 70% of all stockbrokers don't own any stock?"

Please, let's not use the mundane "Are there any questions?" If we have done our homework, we will have planned provocative questions that will be of interest to the audience. Answers to the questions will let you know whether or not your audience understands and agrees.

Don't let your mind trick you into false thinking about the value and importance of questions. For example:

- They're more trouble than they're worth.

  Answer: Not true. It's not a lot of trouble. It is a lot of planning. As for the value—there is no known substitute.

- I just don't have the time. There's too much material to cover.

  Answer: You do have the time. You will do much better to cover less material with questions and discussion than more material without.

- I'm afraid I'll lose control.

  Answer: Not if you do your homework and plan the content and position of each question. What we're looking for is a controlled discussion using questions.

- I'm afraid I'll get into arguments and personality conflicts with loudmouth know-it-alls.

  Answer: Not if you follow the rules of how to handle the trouble-maker.

- I'm more comfortable just giving a straight presentation.

  Answer: You may be. However, the primary objective of your presentation says nothing about your comfort level. You are more likely to achieve your objective if you have interaction with the audience.

There is no better way to get attention and keep interest than a well-thought-out and well-planned question. It is natural for people to want to know the answer to a good question. Questions will also enhance the comprehension and retention of the material.

Questions are just as important to you the presenter. The quality of the answers let you know how effectively you are communicating your message. Areas of misunderstanding are quickly identified.

If the answers to questions in a particular area are consistently vague, or wide off the mark, then you need to either spend more time in that area or, more likely, think of a different conceptual way of presenting the information—such as using an analogy.

Here is something you will run into when giving a presentation to different levels of people within the same organization. People at the bottom of the organizational chart are sometimes reluctant to express an opinion until they know which way the wind is blowing at the top of the organization. So direct a few early questions to the top of the mountain. Make sure they are opinion questions. There are no wrong answers to an opinion question. That will clear the air for the rest of the climbers. Even better is to get the top man to introduce you and the subject and announce his support and endorsement. That guarantees a successful presentation.

ANSWERS

So far we have talked only about questions you would ask of the audience. But what about the other side of the coin? How do we handle questions that are asked of us?

The first thing you must do is create a penalty-free environment for asking questions. The audience must know that it is safe to ask a question. That there will be no ridicule, no rudeness, and no sarcasm. Resist the urge to be witty, clever, humorous or sarcastic in answering questions. Yes, many people will laugh, but you can also make an enemy for life with a clever answer to the wrong person. And remember, no presenter ever won an argument with a client or customer. Never say or do anything that will make the questioner feel stupid or foolish. If in fact they are, let the audience come to that conclusion—not you.

In creating an open and positive environment for questions, our body language speaks louder than our words. For example, if you say, "Are there any questions?" while looking at your notes or down at the floor, your body language says, "I'm not interested in your questions."

In fact, the worst way to start a Q & A is to say, "Are there any questions?" You're likely to get dead silence. A better way would be to ask "Are there any questions about the twelve techniques for getting around a locked-in situation, or about spending a half-day at the Business CIA?" The idea is to jog their memory by focusing their attention to specific subjects. You should then pause, and if there were still no questions, continue by saying, "One of the most frequent questions I get is

_____." If there are still no questions continue by saying, "I am often asked _____."
After you have answered a few of these self-generated questions, I promise you there will be hands in the air to ask questions.

If you genuinely want questions it will be evident to the audience. If you don't, it will be just as evident.

To a large degree you can control the number of questions and the content of the questions. Here's how. At the end of a presentation, when you have some quiet time to yourself, flip back through your cheat sheets and make a note of what questions were asked and where. After you have given the presentation a few times, consistent patterns of questions will begin to develop. It's a simple matter then to incorporate the answers into your presentation. That way, those questions will never be asked.

On the other hand, you might plan on not answering some specific common questions. Then, when the question is asked, you appear to be giving a spontaneous answer. But it is actually a carefully rehearsed response. This is a particularly impressive technique if the answer involves statistics, dates, names, places, and so on, which you have rehearsed and noted on your cheat sheet.

Speaking of rehearsing—why don't you do what the President does? Anticipate the question and rehearse the answer in advance. It works for him for 85% of the questions.

INTERRUPTIONS

What if you are interrupted by a question that will be answered later as a standard part of the presentation? Here are two different approaches to handling that situation.

1. "Betty, I'm coming straight at you with full coverage of that subject in seven minutes."
2. "The answer is *yes* and in just a few minutes we'll get to a complete explanation of why that's so."

Now to some Do's and Don'ts on answering questions.

LISTEN TO THE QUESTION

Carefully. Have you ever been in a meeting where someone asks a question and half way through the question the presenter interrupts the questioner and says, "The answer is so-and-so"? Then the questioner replies, "That was not my question."

What happened here is that the presenter assumed that this question was going to be the same as other questions that had been asked before.

Do not make that mistake. Do not interrupt. Even if you are correct about what the question is, the other members of the audience want and need to hear the complete question.

REPEAT THE QUESTION

If you don't the audience will ask, "What was the question?" If they don't ask it, they will be thinking it. This problem is most common when the question comes from the front of the room. Typically, those in the back of the room can't hear the questions from the front of the room.

In my company when we get a new instructor on board, an experienced instructor will sit in the back of the room for their first few presentations. The experienced instructor will have three pre-printed signs which can be held up as a flag to the new presenter. They say:

"Louder"
"5 Minutes"
"Repeat the Question"

(That tells you the three most common problems with our presenters.)

You want to do more than simply repeat the question. You want to rephrase the question and direct your answer, not to the person who asked it, but to the entire audience. This will enhance the interest of the entire audience in the subject and your answer.

There is a side benefit in this technique. It gives you more thinking time to formulate your answer. We talk slow but the brain is fast. When we rephrase and repeat the question there are a lot of surplus nanoseconds for the brain to organize its answer. So give yourself that extra time. You'll have a better answer.

EYE CONTACT

Look directly at the person while the question is being asked, but when you answer, break eye contact with that person and direct your attention to the entire audience.

ANSWERING MISTAKES

The three most common mistakes in answering questions are:

1.   Answering too much. Keep your answers brief and to the point. If you answer a question with a speech, you sure put a damper on other questions being asked. Long-winded answers are boring, do not help your case, and will cause the audience to tune out.

2.   Answering too soon. This is the interrupt problem we talked about that causes you to answer the wrong question.

3.   Dialogue with one person. Don't allow yourself to fall into a dialogue with one person. Offer to speak with the individual at the end of the program, break eye contact, and move on. If you say, "Does that answer your question?", the most common response is another question.

THE LOADED QUESTION

People have been known to ask loaded or trick questions ("When did you stop beating your wife?"). The first thing to do is state your disagreement with the implied premise —"I have a different view of your implied premise." You can then say, "Therefore I can't answer your question as stated. If, however, what you mean is _____ _____

_____, then my answer would be

_____.

Another approach is to expand the options. If the question asks you to choose between A and B, you can expand the options to include C and D. Then your answer would be choice C or D.

DON'T BLUFF

If you don't know the answer or aren't sure—don't bluff. And don't hesitate, either. If you do, your body language says, "I'm not sure of this answer, but I'm going to try it." Instead be prompt to admit that you do not know the answer. If it's important to the subject at hand then volunteer to find out. Make a written note to yourself (that's important). One effective technique is to reserve a page of a flip chart for questions you are going to follow up. That demonstrates interest and sincerity to the audience.

You can't predict and control everything, but when you operate from a position of full preparation there is nothing wrong with simply answering, "I don't know." As Calvin Coolidge put it, "I have never been hurt by anything I didn't say."

Don't be embarrassed or apologetic about not having all the answers. If you did, you wouldn't be where you are, and you wouldn't be doing what you're doing.

CHAPTER 9

How to Handle Troublemakers

If you have a missionary zeal for one of the controversial, burning issues of our time, then you might want to adopt the philosophy of Albert Einstein when he said, "Great spirits have always encountered violent opposition from mediocre minds."

On the other hand, if most of your presentations are within the happy family of your own company, then your experience may be more like that of Mark Twain when he said, "I've seen a lot of trouble in my time and most of it never happened."

For most of us the reality is somewhere in between. We may find that out of every 100 people there's at least one "nut" or troublemaker. So how do we handle the troublemaker?

LET'S TALK ABOUT TROUBLEMAKERS

First let's talk about what *not* to do. What we should not do are any of those things that are the most natural and instinctive ways to react.

We should not:

- Be defensive and argue with them
- Preach, lecture, or threaten them
- Ignore them
- Criticize them
- Tell them where to go
- Put them down by using ridicule or shame

If you do any of the above, you may feel like you won the battle, but you are likely to lose the war.

Even among fair-minded people, not everyone will want to sing word for word out of our songbook. It's important for us to have a realistic attitude about our audience and our expectations. If we anticipate the troublemaker, we are less likely to come unglued when someone says, "It'll never work." The best way to anticipate the audience is to take the time to get background information on the audience. This will allow you to better understand the opinions, feelings, and biases of those who are likely to disagree with you.

If on the basis of your homework you anticipate disagreement, or if the nature of your subject is somewhat controversial and likely to arouse strong feelings, you should address the disagreement before it addresses you. The best way to ward off trouble is to head it off at the pass. The way we do that is to recognize in our early remarks that there are some other points of view on this subject. Then—and this is important—you state in summary form the other point of view. If you are the one who brings it up, you can explain it in your words and within the context of the view you are going to present. That will burst the balloon of the hostile troublemaker. You have stated his case for him and thereby taken the sting out of his comments. The audience will appreciate the fairness and evenhandedness of recognizing other points of view. The bottom line effect of this is to lend credibility and strength to your case.

We will now categorize the troublemakers and talk further about techniques of neutralizing, defusing, and minimizing their effect.

THE HOSTILE TROUBLEMAKER

He is the worst of all. He or she is the one who'll burst out with statements like, "That'll never happen"; "It'll never work"; "I don't agree." His remarks may even take the form of a personal attack on you or what you represent.

One strategy for handling the hostile troublemaker is to persuade the rest of the audience to your way of thinking before the troublemaker can do his damage. The way we do this is to preface our presentation with a remark like the following: "For the next 30 minutes I am going to present a new concept. I would like to ask that we just have an open mind and hold our comments or questions until I finish. Is that all right?" Of course the group will agree that it's all right. Then if the troublemaker tries to interrupt we can merely refer to the agreement of the group to hold comments until we finish the presentation of the new concept. If you followed the Presentation Planning Guide in Chapter 16 you will have persuaded the audience to your view. If the troublemaker now makes a statement like, "It'll never work," he will tend to be put down by the audience and viewed as not having an open mind. And rather than you responding to the troublemaker's comment, it's more effective if you let another member of the audience respond. Now his or her disagreement is not with you, but with the rest of the audience. That's like a hammer to the head. The message to the troublemaker is, "You're outnumbered and you've got it wrong."

Another way of defusing the troublemaker is to use the weight-of-evidence technique. Since you know what you are going to present, you will also know the more common objections. That being the case, you can prepare yourself in advance with facts, figures, references, quotes, and so forth for the common objections. The strategy is to drown the troublemaker with the weight of the evidence you have prepared or collected. He is disadvantaged since he is not as prepared as you are for an intelligent discussion. Your dialogue might sound like this: "You may be right, but let me review the facts and the evidence that supports my position." You can now, once again, turn to the audience for support.

Hostile questions sometimes have hostile words imbedded in the question. Words like rip-off, sneaky, hedging. You can defuse these words by asking for clarification. Do not repeat hostile words when you rephrase the questions. In fact, a truly hostile question that is loaded with emotion should not be repeated. Approach it instead as follows: "I can't answer your entire question. If, however, what you mean by _____ is _____ then my answer is _____." Or, "If what you would like to know is__ , then my answer is _____." Clearly state your position but do not let the interrogator goad you into a debate or an emotional argument. Again, it's far better to ask for input from someone in the audience whom you know does not agree with the opinion of the troublemaker.

Another way of handling troublemakers is to let them destroy themselves. You do this by answering a hostile question with a question. "If you feel that way about the situation, then what do you think should be done to correct it?" The answers to these kinds of questions tend to be recognized by the audience as more emotional than well-thought-out, logical answers. The longer he talks the more the troublemaker hurts himself. It starts to become apparent that he has an ax to grind.

Negative comments or questions are not always hostile. Some people just like to argue or play the devil's advocate. You know the type. You say it's hot, they say it's cold. Their comments or questions tend to be nit-picking, directing attention away from your central point. The strategy here is to get their agreement on the larger point. You can then respond with, "Although we may have a difference on the detail, we're in agreement on the concept."

Finally, don't lose your cool. Avoid eye contact with the troublemaker. The more visual contact you have with the troublemaker, the more irritated you will become. If all else fails, just say, "It looks like we have different views on this subject. Why don't we discuss it in more detail after the meeting?" Strange thing. Rarely do they want to discuss the subject after the meeting. They seem to be more interested in a verbal interchange in front of an audience. Guess that tells us something about the troublemaker.

THE KNOW-IT-All TROUBLEMAKER

This one has a club they use to intimidate people. Some types of clubs are:

- Length of service
- Advanced degree
- Experience
- Title
- Professional status

Their remarks are prefaced with:

- "In my 20 years of experience. . . ."
- "I have a Ph.D. in Economics and. . . ."
- "I have worked on this project more than anyone in the room and. . . ."
- "As a senior systems analyst my opinion is. . . ."

The unstated assumption here is that he knows more than you do, hence he is right and you are wrong.

The key to handling the know-it-all is to stick to the facts. Do not theorize or speculate. Stick to your own experiences and well-documented evidence. People can legitimately question and disagree with your theory or your speculation. But they cannot question your experience or documented facts.

Another way of handling the know-it-all troublemaker is to use quotes of other experts whose credentials are even greater than those of the troublemaker.

Let me tell you another approach I stumbled on by accident. Often you know in advance or can find out in advance if you are going to have any know-it-alls in the audience. Arrange a meeting with them in advance. Acknowledge their credentials. Tell them what you are going to present and ask for their support. You will be amazed more often than not to find that they will support and endorse your program. So what started out to be a problem has now become a reference.

Let's take the worst case scenario. Suppose the know-it-all will not support you. You can still take the sting out of his punch by announcing in advance that you and he do not agree and here's why. You are stating his case for him and thereby defusing him.

THE LOUDMOUTH TROUBLEMAKER

This is the person who talks too much, too loud, dominates the meeting, and seems impossible to shut up.

The most subtle techniques for coping with loudmouths involve your physical position in relation to them. Try moving closer and closer to them while they are talking and maintain eye contact until you are standing right in front of them. Your physical presence—you are standing, they are sitting—will often make them aware of their behavior and they will stop talking.

Here are some other techniques for dealing with loudmouths:

- Interrupt them with the question, "What would you say is your main point?"
- Make eye contact with the loudmouth and say, "I appreciate your comments, but we would like to also hear from other people."
- After a reasonable amount of time ask the loudmouth, "What is your question?"
- Questions that are vague, open-ended, or not relevant can be answered as follows:
  —"I'm not qualified to give you an intelligent answer to that question."
  —"That's a good question, but in the short time we have I would like to stick to the subject of _____."
  —"Interesting point, but how does it relate to the subject of _____?
- Avoid eye contact and conveniently don't see their hands.
- Ask them to record, take notes, or list questions and "to-dos" for follow-up. (That will keep them busy.)
- Finally, during a coffee break you can recognize their interest in the subject, but tell them you are running behind because of the open discussion, and ask for their support in keeping the discussion down. You could even suggest they jot down questions they would like to discuss with you after the meeting.

THE INTERRUPTER TROUBLEMAKER

This type starts talking before others are finished. Often, the interrupter doesn't mean to be rude, but becomes impatient and overly excited. Like the loudmouth, the interrupter is afraid that a new, red-hot idea will be lost if it isn't blurted out immediately.

There is a simple and easy solution to the interrupter. Every time they start doing it, jump in and say, "Wait a minute Jim, let's let John finish what he was saying." After you do this a few times the interrupter will get the message.

THE INTERPRETER TROUBLEMAKER

They continually want to speak for other people. They can always be recognized by the phrase "What John is really trying to say is...," or "What I hear John saying is...."

The first part of our solution is the same as for the interrupter. If John is still in the middle of talking we want to jump in quickly and say, "Wait a minute, let's let John speak for himself. Go ahead, John, finish what you were saying."

If John has already finished talking, then turn to him and ask, "John, do you think Jim correctly understood what you said? Was his interpretation an accurate representation of what you were saying?"

A couple of these will cure the interpreter real quick.

THE GOSSIPER TROUBLEMAKERS

They introduce gossip, rumors, and hearsay into the discussion. Valuable time can be wasted arguing over whether something is true or not.

"Isn't there a regulation that you can't...?"

"It seems like I remember that...."

"I thought I heard so and so say...."

Immediately ask if anyone can confirm or verify the accuracy of the statement. If they cannot, then give the ball back to the gossiper with the statement, "Let's not take the time of the group until we can verify the accuracy of the information."

THE WHISPERER TROUBLEMAKER

Nothing is more irritating to a presenter than two people whispering while you are presenting. There are four solutions.

One is to walk up close to the whisperers and make eye contact with them. Another is to stop talking and establish dead silence. When you do, what was a whisper becomes a roar—and an embarrassment to the whisperers.

A third approach is to call one of them by name and ask, "Do you have something you would like to share with the group?" Or finally, you can ask a question and then call on them by name. It's hard to come up with the right answer when you don't even know the question. They aren't likely to want a repeat of that embarrassment.

THE SILENT TROUBLEMAKER

They sit in the back of the room, don't say anything, may be reading a newspaper, rolling their eyes, shaking their heads, crossing and uncrossing legs, pushing their chair back from the table, and so forth. In many ways they are the most difficult of all. At least with the overtalkative participants, you know where you stand. With the silent treatment, you don't know if they understand what you're talking about, aren't interested, are thinking about something else, are shy and unassertive, aren't interested in the subject, don't like you, or what.

The only real weapon you have for silent troublemakers is the Rifleshot Question. Call them by name, then follow with an open question that calls for an opinion, an experience, an example, and so on.

The other thing you can do is talk to them at the break on a personal basis about the subject, their understanding, their questions, their agreement or disagreement, or what have you.

In presentations, as in life, the silent treatment can be the worst. And as in life, there are no magic answers, just a need for patience and tolerance.

THE BUSY-BUSY TROUBLEMAKERS

They are always ducking in and out of the meeting, constantly receiving messages or rushing out to take a phone call, or deal with a crisis. What's worse, the busy-busy is often the manager or senior person in the meeting.

That's why he or she feels so free to come and go. But by doing so, the busy-busy ends up wasting his or her time, and the time of the rest of the participants. During each departure, the meeting may come to a standstill. Or the busy-busy has to be briefed upon reentry. Often there is no point in continuing a meeting if a key person is absent.

Here are some ways of dealing with the busy-busy troublemaker.

1. The simplest and most effective way is to hold the presentation on your turf or neutral turf, and not his home ground. That way you remove him from his support systems, and you will be in control of the messages.

2. Another solution is to schedule the presentation either before or after normal business hours.

3. If you have to give the presentation on his turf, then you can announce in advance the time and duration of the break for coffee and phone calls. He will usually get the message.

4. Sometimes you will know in advance that you will have this problem because you know the individual. If that's the case then go to Mr. or Ms. Busy-Busy and tell him or her that you want to schedule the presentation on a date and time they will be able to attend with minimum interruption. Again, they will usually get the message.

THE LATECOMER TROUBLEMAKER

This is a tough one, but here are some thoughts:

- Pick an odd time for the meeting or presentation to start. Don't pick 8:30 or 9:00. Have it announced and publicized that the presentation will start at 8:47. That kind of a start time is a tip-off to the attendees that this meeting is probably really going to start at 8:47.

- You can also have it announced and publicized that a door prize will be awarded at 8:48. The value of the door prize is not important. It can even be a novelty item.

THE EARLY-LEAVER TROUBLEMAKER

- Make remarks to the latecomer only if it feels natural and comfortable for your body chemistry. And smile when you make them, such as "I'm sorry, I must have started early."

- Stop talking and establish dead silence while the latecomer makes his way to a seat.

- Establish a late kitty. Anyone late for a meeting has to put a quarter or a dollar in the late kitty (used for coffee and rolls).

- Announce to the latecomer that she has been volunteered to do some follow-up staff work.

THE EARLY-LEAVER TROUBLEMAKER

Few things are more disconcerting to a presenter than someone standing up and walking out in the middle of the presentation.

The best way to stop this is to get agreement in advance that it will not happen. You can do this by announcing the time that the presentation will be over, and then asking if anyone has a problem with that schedule. If no one says anything, then we have established a gentlemen's agreement. A potential early-leaver would be pretty embarrassed to walk out after that.

If anyone does state they cannot stay for the entire presentation, he or she will usually volunteer a legitimate reason.

In summary, the best antidote for a troublemaker is a well-prepared and well-rehearsed presentation that anticipates objections and conflicting points of view. If we build the answers into our presentation we will earn high marks from the audience for fairness and completeness, and have silenced the troublemaker by singing his song for him—but to our own tune.

Rehearse, Rehearse
Rehearse—Then Cheat

Good presenters communicate the feeling that they are comfortable, relaxed, in command of the situation, know what they are talking about, and enjoy doing what they are doing.

Are they born that way? Do they just wake up one morning with those traits? How does it happen? I suggest to you that one becomes a good presenter the same way one becomes a good golfer, a good cabinetmaker, or a good lawyer. By preparation, by practice, and by doing.

The good golfer makes it look so easy. The smooth swing, the distance, the accuracy. More than easy, it looks effortless. But behind that superb coordination of mind and muscle are years of work, practice, and a few gallons of sweat. There is no easy and painless path to golfing goodness. And there is no fast-food route to becoming a good presenter. You have to pay your dues. It's like that question, "How do you get to Carnegie Hall?" Answer: "Practice, practice, practice."

And so it is with the presenter. The good ones make it look so easy, so natural. They appear calm, composed, and confident. They come through to the audience as having warmth, authority, and sincerity. But behind that appearance are hours of preparation, practice, and doing. Preparation and practice will more than compensate for any lack of talent.

Would you think making a presentation is more of an art or more like a science? Most people would agree that it is more like an art. That being the case, as is true of all forms of art, you improve with practice. And the *only* way to improve is by practice.

There are two compelling reasons for you to rehearse. The first is that it is the single best solution to the problem of tight nerves and sweaty palms. You have good reason to be nervous and sweaty if you don't know what you're going to say, or how you're going to say it. The concept of, "I'll play it by ear" is a guarantee of mediocrity at best.

The second reason for rehearsing is even more important than the first. It has to do with achieving your objective. Let's suppose that the objective of the presentation is to sell something. Let's further suppose that on a scale from zero to 100% that your presentation effectiveness is 50% and your competitor's effectiveness is 100%. Are you going to get 50% of the business? Absolutely not. You are going to get zero. Your competitor is going to get all the business. Every time you do battle with that competitor you are going to lose. The win/lose decision is not an analogue decision—it is binary. Most prospects or clients are not in the business of helping the needy. A very important key to being a winner on the competitive battlefield is to give an effective presentation. Some say it is the *most* important key.

What about price? Isn't the low bidder always the winner? If that were true, we could eliminate a few million sales jobs. The average American spends over 50% more money for a new car than is necessary if price were the primary buying criteria. Some spend 100% or more. I did it myself.

So if you could use a little more business, get your act together, do your homework and rehearse, rehearse, rehearse. If you don't, your audience will know you haven't. That sends them a strong message that says, "I don't think you're very important. If you were I'd be better prepared." Remember, the quality of your presentation is a mirror image of the quality of your product, your service, your support, and your people.

Let's talk about a few specifics. If you have not rehearsed—if you are not sure what you are going to say, and you have to switch your brain into a deep-think mode to think up what you're going to say next in front of the audience—then you cannot have good eye contact with the audience. It is impossible to have eye contact while in deep-think mode. If you are in deep thought, what are you looking at? You are looking at the floor, the ceiling, or out into space with glazed-over eyes.

Another example. We have talked about the importance of a pleasant facial expression—specifically, a smile. If you have not rehearsed, you're not sure what you're going to say next. If you have to switch into deep-think mode to think up what you're going to say next, what is going to be the expression of your face? Not only will it not be a smile, it will be a frown. Nothing could be worse. It is impossible to smile and deep-think at the same time. And by the way, what do you think would be the tone of your voice? You've got it—a monotone.

A major problem with presenters is that they are so content-oriented, so absorbed in what they are saying, that they are oblivious to how they appear to the audience. If you have glazed-over eyes, a frown on your face, and are speaking in a monotone, the quality of your content is irrelevant. There is no way you can keep the attention and interest of the audience and achieve your objective. As we said earlier, 55% of the impact of your presentation is nonverbal communications.

The only way you can concentrate on your voice, your facial expression, and have eye contact with the audience, is to have a free mind to concentrate on those items. The only way you can have a free mind is to know in advance what you are going to say. The only way you can do that is to rehearse.

There is a right way and a wrong way to rehearse. The wrong way is to just flip through your visuals and glance at your cheat sheets.

HOW TO REHEARSE

The right way to rehearse is to duplicate the conditions of your presentations. That means rehearsing in the actual room using the actual visual aids, going through the actual movements, gestures, and saying the actual words. If it's not practical to rehearse in the actual room, then use one as similar as possible. There is no substitute for doing the real thing, the real way. If you don't, I assure you there will be some surprises in store for you when you are standing in front of a live audience. And the last thing you want or need is a surprise.

If your rehearsal can be made to some friends or colleagues, so much the better. They can observe what you can't see—how you will look and sound to your audience.

If your presentation involves writing on a flip chart or a board, be sure to include that in your rehearsal. This will allow you to solve in advance the problems of:

- Spelling
- Positioning
- Running off the page
- Running out of paper
- Out-of-ink Magic Marker
- No chalk
- Lettering too small
- Poor drawing

- Out of scale
- No color
- No erasers

That gives us an idea of the things that can go wrong—and that's just in one area. There are three important things to remember. The first is, there is no substitute for a dress rehearsal. The second is, there is no substitute for a dress rehearsal. And the third is, there is no substitute for a dress rehearsal.

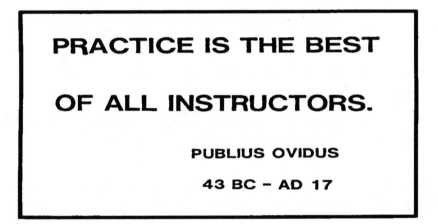

PRACTICE IS THE BEST

OF ALL INSTRUCTORS.

PUBLIUS OVIDUS

43 BC – AD 17

FIGURE 10A Some things never change

The ultimate fear of all presenters is not that they will stumble and fumble (bad as that is) through a presentation, but that they will be standing in front of an audience and suddenly go blank. Some even have dreams about that and wake up in a cold sweat.

If we use cheat sheets, that will never happen. The purpose of the cheat sheet is to guide us step-by-step through the presentation. It gives us key words and phrases; questions to ask; and miniature drawings of pictures, graphs, schematics, and so on. It has the first three to five words we will say for each key point. It is a shorthand script of the presentation and tells us what to do and when.

If we have done a proper job of rehearsing, we will have become very familiar with our cheat sheets and the material they contain. A quick glance at a cheat sheet tells you where you are and what comes next. With practice, one glance will carry you for a minute or two. What happens here is that when you glance at the cheat sheet you pick up the first three to five words. Then when you say those words, if you have properly rehearsed, the follow-on words and explanation will flow smoothly.

A strange thing will happen after you have given a presentation a few times. Your mind will start to form a mental image of the cheat sheet. Next thing you know you will be able to see the cheat sheets in your mind. At a minimum, one quick glance at a cheat sheet will bring a recall of the entire page.

This gives you the reality of the dream of all presenters:

- You have the power and drama of key words and phrases.

- The surrounding words flow automatically and smoothly.

- You convey the appearance of giving an effective and exciting presentation extemporaneously and from memory.

For an actual example of how to use a cheat sheet, turn back to Chapter 6 (Getting Attention and Keeping Interest) and look at Figure 6C. When I am giving my presentation entitled "Presenting, Persuading, and Winning," I draw that figure in real time on a flip chart as I describe it. If you start reading just after Figure 6C, you will hear me talking and see me drawing. The cheat sheet I use for this little exercise is Figure 10B. Notice the use of key words and phrases to guide me through the presentation. You will never go blank and never be at a loss for words if you use cheat sheets.

The happy face in the bottom right is to remind me to smile. Right under it, the TC-15 is my time check. This tells me that when I get to this place in the presentation I should have taken 15 minutes. If I have taken 20 minutes to get to this point, then I know I am 5 minutes behind schedule. I would then exercise my action plan as described in Chapter 14 (Time Control).

The large drawing at the bottom tells me what my finished product should look like as I draw it in three stages, as shown on the right side of the page.

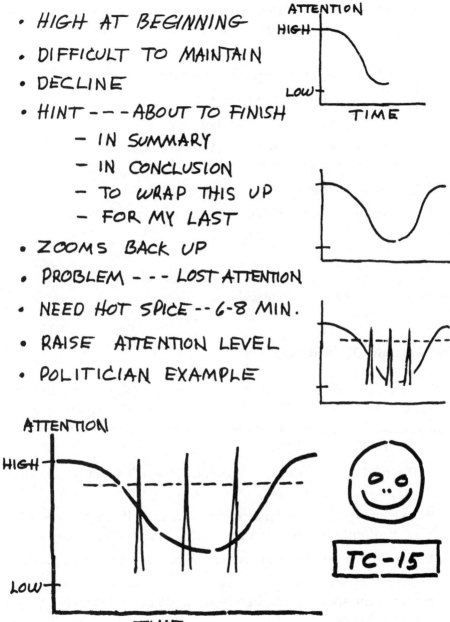

- HIGH AT BEGINNING
- DIFFICULT TO MAINTAIN
- DECLINE
- HINT – – – ABOUT TO FINISH
    - IN SUMMARY
    - IN CONCLUSION
    - TO WRAP THIS UP
    - FOR MY LAST
- ZOOMS BACK UP
- PROBLEM – – – LOST ATTENTION
- NEED HOT SPICE – – 6-8 MIN.
- RAISE ATTENTION LEVEL
- POLITICIAN EXAMPLE

FIGURE 10B Sample of a cheat sheet.

Cheat sheets take many forms and different media depending on the presenter and his or her choice of visual aids. For example:

- Around the sides of frames used for transparencies
- Lightly written and drawn on flip charts
- A page underneath each transparency
- Flip frames (side panel attached to a transparency that folds out and functions as frame and as cheat sheets)
- On the back of the previous page of a flip chart
- A cheat sheet page per slide or even multiple slides per page

Often no cheat sheet is necessary since the content of many of your visuals will be their own cheat sheet.

WHAT CAN GO WRONG

In "Hot Drugs for Sweaty Palms" (Chapter 3) we suggested that you arrive one hour early. Believe me, you will be glad you did. Here are some of the things that can and will go wrong:

- The cord of your visual aid equipment won't reach the electrical outlet.
- You finally get an extension cord but your three-pronged plug won't fit into the two-pronged holes of the extension cord.
- The light control for your room is on the other side of the partition in another room.
- There is no space beside the overhead projector for you to lay your transparencies.
- The make and model of the projector works very differently from the one you're accustomed to.

- The flip-chart stand is not designed for your flip-chart paper.
- On the hotel's announcement board the name of your program is misspelled and the start time is not correct.
- It's Monday morning and the air conditioning to your room was turned off over the weekend and somebody forgot to turn it back on this morning.
- The microphone makes a high-pitched noise.
- The screen is too small.
- They are repainting the stripes in the parking lot so there's no place for the attendees to park.
- The phone in the back of the room is ringing off the hook.

Well, you get the idea. And this is not fiction. All of the above have happened to me.

You can avoid these kind of problems by doing a good job of planning and communicating with the host, coordinator, leader, or whoever is in charge. Leave nothing to chance. Review your requirements in advance and in detail. The last thing you want or need is a surprise.

CHECKLIST

The following is a combination checklist for planning and a "To Do" list when you arrive. The single most important item is "Who to call for help." You need the name, availability, and number of someone who has the authority and the wherewithal to "fix things" on short notice. In fact, I would recommend that you have that person meet you in the room when you arrive one hour early. If there isn't something that needs fixing or changing, it will be a miracle.

I learned the value of a checklist from my jet fighter pilot days. I can tell you that no pilot is going to strap-on to a blow torch without a checklist, and you shouldn't grab on to a podium without one either.

You may not need to know how to recover from a "flame-out" at 40,000 feet, but the burnout of a projector bulb, and the absence of a spare, can also cause stark terror.

I have three checklists:

- A packing checklist for out of town travel
- A checklist for each of my presentations and seminars
- An on-site checklist

I suggest you make your own checklist that's specifically tailored to your needs and your presentation. The following can get you started.

Facilities

_____   Who to call for help and the phone number (home and office)

_____   Restroom location

_____   Phone location

_____   Snacks location

_____   Stairs/elevators location

_____   Fire alarm procedures

_____   Signs for directions to meeting

_____   Parking accommodations

_____   Location of copy machine

_____   Phone number for messages

Room

_____   Check light controls and set level

_____   Temperature controls

_____   Disconnect phone in room

_____ Smokers' considerations

_____ Chairs/tables arrangement

_____ Extension cord

_____ Pencil sharpener

_____ Electrical cords taped down

_____ Coat rack

_____ Lectern

_____ Water pitcher and glasses

_____ Location of electrical outlets

_____ Adapter plug—three-prong to two-prong

_____ Position of spotlights

Overhead Projector

_____ Spare bulb

_____ Focused

_____ Cleaned of fingerprints and lint

_____ First transparency in place

Slide Projector

_____ Spare bulb

_____ Focused

_____ Tray cued to slot one

_____ Opaque slide in slot one

Movie Projector

_____ Check bulb

_____ Focused and set to fill screen

_____   Sound level check

_____   Film cued up to title frame

Music

_____   Cued

_____   Sound level check

Screen

_____   Location

_____   Size

Flip Chart

_____   Paper supply

_____   Magic Markers

_____   Check for dry ink in markers

_____   Rubber band across top

Videotape

_____   Check out control

_____   Tape cued

_____   Sound level set

High Tech and Computer Driven

_____   Arrive two hours early

_____   Technician on standby

_____   Back-up or bypass alternatives

Microphone

_____   Lavaliere attachment

_____   Extra cord length for movement

_____   Sound check

_____   Back-up mike

Board

_____   Chalk

_____   Eraser

_____   Clean

Refreshments

_____   Coffee

_____   Decaffeinated

_____   Tea

_____   Juice

_____   Soft drinks

_____   Other

Audience Supplies

_____   Note pads

_____   Pencils

_____   Handouts

_____   Place cards

_____   Badges

_____   Roster

_____   Agenda

Final Mini-Rehearsal

_____   Opening

_____   Sequence check

_____   Close

I'm not suggesting that you do all this work yourself. But what you must do is have crystal clear communications with the meeting planner. Figure 10C is the support requirement checklist I send to the meeting planner 30 days in advance of my Presentations Plus Workshop. What you must do is arrive early and *inspect* what you *expect*.

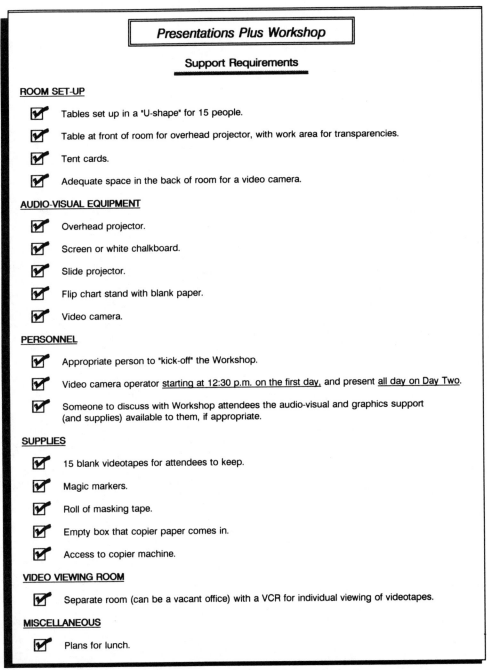

Presentations Plus Workshop

Support Requirements

ROOM SET-UP

- ☑ Tables set up in a "U-shape" for 15 people.
- ☑ Table at front of room for overhead projector, with work area for transparencies.
- ☑ Tent cards.
- ☑ Adequate space in the back of room for a video camera.

AUDIO-VISUAL EQUIPMENT

- ☑ Overhead projector.
- ☑ Screen or white chalkboard.
- ☑ Slide projector.
- ☑ Flip chart stand with blank paper.
- ☑ Video camera.

PERSONNEL

- ☑ Appropriate person to "kick-off" the Workshop.
- ☑ Video camera operator <u>starting at 12:30 p.m. on the first day,</u> and present <u>all day on Day Two</u>.
- ☑ Someone to discuss with Workshop attendees the audio-visual and graphics support (and supplies) available to them, if appropriate.

SUPPLIES

- ☑ 15 blank videotapes for attendees to keep.
- ☑ Magic markers.
- ☑ Roll of masking tape.
- ☑ Empty box that copier paper comes in.
- ☑ Access to copier machine.

VIDEO VIEWING ROOM

- ☑ Separate room (can be a vacant office) with a VCR for individual viewing of videotapes.

MISCELLANEOUS

- ☑ Plans for lunch.

Figure 10C Checklist for meeting planner. *Inspect* what you *expect.*

Bad habits, mannerisms, and other distractions can literally *destroy* a presentation that has a good opening, a powerful close, is well organized, has excellent visual aids, lots of Hot Spice, and is delivered with enthusiasm.

As we get into specifics you are going to think, "That's really nit-picking," but a presentation is the sum of a thousand nits. And just as a drop of dye can turn an entire glass of water murky, so, too, can a single distracting mannerism turn a good presentation very sour very fast. Once you've turned them off, you'll never get them back. If the guys in the back row have money on the table and are keeping score on the number of "ahs," "uhs," or ear lobe pulls, then you have lost the game. Nonverbal communications is strong medicine. What we do can speak much louder than what we say. For example: If you stand up in front of an audience with a frown on your face, look down at the floor, and say, "I'm really excited to be here," the immediate interpretation is—"You lie." Your body language and your voice can reinforce your words or destroy your message. Your visual and auditory clues tell the audience more clearly how you feel about the subject than do your words. A presenter who talks in a monotone, has a frozen stance, and an absence of enthusiasm, is saying, "Take it or leave it."

Let's talk about some of the components of body language and voice.

POSTURE

Some distracting characteristics are:

- Slouching
- Speaking with head bowed
- Hanging on to supports for dear life: lectern, flip-chart stand, table, and so on
- Rigid—like a military position
- Rocking from side to side or
- Rocking front to back—heel to toe

Sometimes there are posture characteristics that seem to go with certain jobs.

One time I was down in Florida making a presentation to a conference on "How to Give an Effective Presentation." I was speaking to the point of posture characteristics that seem to go with certain jobs, and I used the example of managers in IBM. I demonstrated a common characteristic of IBM managers—which is to unbutton the jacket, put both hands in the pants pockets, and bounce up and down on the balls of the feet.

Well, the next morning was the wrap-up of the conference. Unknown to me, the final speaker was a big, *big* shot from IBM HQ. This was a big deal. With 500 people in the audience he walks out on the stage, unbuttons his jacket, puts both hands in his pants pockets, and says, "Good morning, ladies and gentlemen" while bouncing up and down on the balls of his feet. Well, this broke the audience up. Of course, he didn't know what was going on. As the audience was laughing you could see stark terror on his face as he looked down to see if his fly was unzipped. Well, that really broke the audience up. Afterward somebody told him what had happened. He sent me to Alaska. Took me two years to get back.

SMOKING AND DRINKING

I bet you've been in meetings where the presenter was sipping coffee and/or smoking a cigarette while trying to present.

Let me just make a flat statement on that subject. *Don't do it.* Not only is it distracting—it's bad manners.

FACIAL EXPRESSION

If you walk down the street and just look at the expressions on people's faces, you rarely see a smile. Mostly you see a deadpan or severe look— sometimes a scowling or an apathetic expression. You don't want to be caught in front of an audience looking like that. What's the answer? The answer is to smile. But most of us forget to smile. The solution is to write the word "SMILE" in red on about every fourth cheat sheet. Just looking at the word will cause you to smile.

GUARANTEED DISTRACTIONS

Here are some bad habits that are guaranteed to take the mind of the audience off the subject. These are like drops of dirty dye in the clear water of your presentation.

- Rattling keys or coins in your pocket
- The habitual and continuing use of "uhs" or "ahs." Some people double-clutch it and say "uh-uh" or "ah-ah."
- Sucking the teeth
- Ring twisting
- Stroking a beard
- Lip licking
- Tugging your ear
- Lip biting
- Cracking knuckles
- Pushing the bridge of your glasses
- Playing with a watch
- Drumming your finger
- Bouncing a pencil on its eraser
- Blowing hair out of your eyes
- Popping the top of a Magic Marker
- Extending and retracting a telescoping pointer

Women, in particular, should look out for:

- Twirling hair
- Playing with beads, gold chains, or other jewelry

Let me ask you a question. If you had any of these bad habits, do you think you would be aware of them? Probably not. For example, I know a lady who did a lot of presentations on a particular subject. She was excellent. No one had more experience or knew the subject better. There was just one problem. She had a bad habit. She used a flip chart in her presentation, so she always had a Magic Marker in her hand. Her bad habit was the popping of the top of the Magic Marker about every ten seconds.

Well, the popping of the top of a Magic Marker doesn't make a very loud noise, but if you're doing it every ten seconds that's six times a minute, or 360 times an hour. By the time you get up to pop number 125, they start to sound like rifle shots.

Do you think she was aware of what she was doing? Did she hear the noise? Absolutely not. But to the audience that sound became magnified 20-fold. And, ironically, your best friends will rarely tell you. What to do? Coming shortly.

EYE CONTACT

This is a way for you to say to every person in the audience, "You are important. I'm talking just to you."

And yet, too often the presenter will focus on the floor or the ceiling, tend to look at the same two or three people, or stare over the heads of the audience. Sometimes the presenter will have a visual obsession with one side of the room to the exclusion of the other.

Lack of eye contact gives the impression that you are talking at people instead of to people.

There is another important reason for eye contact. It is the source of feedback that tells you how you're doing. Are they with you? Do they understand? Do they agree? Are you moving too fast? Are you belaboring a point? You will never know if you don't look at them.

For small groups you can have eye contact with every person multiple times. But it doesn't happen automatically. It requires a conscious and planned effort on your part. For a large audience you can create the illusion of individual contact by focusing on a few specific people in various parts of the room. Focus on one, then sweep your eyes slowly to the next one. Don't throw darting glances. And don't forget the people on the extreme right and left or those in the last three rows.

MOVEMENT

What can be worse than a presenter who is frozen in one spot?

Answer: One who runs back and forth across the front of the room like a caged animal. We want and need movement, but it needs to be planned, deliberate, and controlled—not that of a lion in a cage.

GESTURES

Gestures are like movement. The only thing worse than none is too many. And as with movement, gestures should be smooth, deliberate, and natural. The purpose of gestures is to accent and reinforce your message. Please don't look like Robinson Crusoe waving at a passing plane.

DRESS

Entire books are written on this subject, but everything we need to know can be summarized in ten seconds.

1. Do not wear clothes that talk louder than you do. When your attire competes with your message for the attention of the audience—you lose.

2. And for you women—nothing too bright, too tight, too low or too short.

3. And you guys—button your coat. I know that sounds like a nit, but it makes a difference and it sends a signal. You'll never see a pro with an open coat.

4. Here's an answer that always works. Dress like you're going to a funeral and you'll have it just right.

And get a haircut—increase your odds of success by 24 percent.

VOICE

The dominant source of input to human beings is visual. You would think the dominant source of output would be the spoken word. It is, but that's not the whole truth. How you say something can be more dominant than what you say.

Have you ever had a spat with your spouse, not over what was said but because of the manner or tone in which it was spoken? Just as we read between the lines we also listen between the words—not for *what* was said, but for *how* it was said.

For example, you can say the same words and convey three different messages:

- I really believe in what I'm saying.
- I don't have a lot of knowledge or experience on this subject.
- I don't care what you think, I'm just doing my job.

Some of the problems with the voice are:

- Monotone
- High pitch
- Volume drop at end of sentences
- Inaudibility
- Lack of variety in pace or volume
- Nasal sound
- Mumbling

These all fall under one or more of the four characteristics of the human voice: pitch, loudness, rate, and quality.

Pitch What we want to avoid is the monotony of the same pitch. What we want are variations or inflections.

Loudness Speaking too loudly is almost as bad as speaking too softly. You will have just the right volume if you imagine that you are talking to the people seated near the rear of the room. But remember, we need variations in loudness. Dropping the voice to a near whisper can be as effective for emphasis as raising it to a near shout. Some of both will do the job. Avoid the monotony of unvarying sound. It's wearing on the listener.

Rate Speaking too fast for too long inhibits effective communication. On the other hand, if you talk too slowly you will put people to sleep. The magic words are variety, change of pace, and pause. Failure to use the pause is one of the more common mistakes of presenters.

The master of pace and pause is the news commentator Paul Harvey. Rapid-fire words followed by a pause followed by a few seconds of slow pace is his effective technique. If you calculated the number of words per minute he speaks, they would be about the average of most speakers. But what a difference the peaks, valleys, and pauses make in the attentiveness of the audience. The right formula is fast, pause, slow.

Quality There are great differences in the quality of the voice of singers and of speakers. The quality of your voice is directly affected by your knowledge, confidence, and belief in the subject. If you suspect that you might have a problem with the quality of your voice, you will find the answer in the chapter "Rehearse, Rehearse, Rehearse—Then Cheat."

Words, Phrases, and Pronunciation A kissin' cousin to problems of voice characteristics is the use of certain words and phrases that detract from the effectiveness of presentations. We have already mentioned the "um's" and the "uh's," but there are others like:

- "Y'know"
- "Okay, okay"
- "Kind of"

- "Sort of"
- "Wonderful, wonderful"
- "You know what I mean?"

If you're not sure how to pronounce a word, either don't use it, or look it up. Pronunciation errors are often perceived by the listener as an indication of ignorance and poor preparation. Some people will automatically put you in the uneducated category if you use a word like "irregardless." What would they think if you said something like, "Git your camera out and take a pitcher of the athelete."

As we said, if you have some bad habits and distractions, you may be the last to know. Your best friend won't tell you. They have learned that there are few things in life more unwanted than unsolicited advice. So how are you going to find out?

The best way of all is to see yourself the way other people see you. That means videotape. If you ever have the opportunity to have yourself videotaped, don't pass it up. There is absolutely nothing as effective in dramatically hammering home your distracting habits as a videotape. It can be a humbling but invaluable experience—so brace yourself. On the other hand, if your name is Clarence Darrow or William Jennings Bryan, you can sit back and see how great you really are.

If you don't have access to a videotape machine, there are two other things you can do.

Borrow a cassette tape recorder and capture the vocal part of the presentation. This will let you hear what the audience hears. If you speak in a monotone with no change of pace or pitch, it will be immediately obvious.

The next thing you can do is to have a friend or colleague sit in the back as an observer, and critique you. Pick this person carefully.

He or she should be someone whose judgment you respect and whom you believe will be objective and candid. Your spouse is not a good candidate. Give them a critique sheet to follow. (See "Getting Good, Getting Better—The Critique.") Ask them to note your strengths as well as your weaknesses. We are interested in improving our style, not destroying our confidence.

MISCELLANEOUS BUT IMPORTANT DISTRACTIONS

These distractions are listed last, but they can blow you out of the water as fast as anything else.

Misspelled Words

People will think that if you're sloppy with your spelling, then you'll also be sloppy with your service or support.

Fancy Talk

Complex subjects require complex language. Right? Wrong! Your success is determined by how well you are understood—not by the size of your vocabulary. And don't use acronyms unless you're 100% sure they're understood by everyone in the audience. If a few acronyms are central to your presentation, then use them but define them before you do.

Talking to the Board

Do not talk to the screen, board, or flip charts. Watch the weather reporter on TV. Note how she describes the weather without talking to the screen.

Playing With Objects

If you continue to hold any kind of object (pointer, pencil, Magic Marker, chalk, etc.) in your hand, I promise you that it's just a matter of time before you start playing with it. If your pointer becomes a baton and you look like you're conducting the symphony, your audience is likely to be preoccupied with your direction to the bass section and not the content of your presentation.

Here's the solution. Any time you pick up any object, use it for the purpose for which you picked it up, then immediately put it down. Never hold anything in your hand that you're not using.

Off-Center Projection

Now here is a real nit, but believe me, it can really irritate an audience. A simple little thing like centering the picture on the screen. Strange things can preoccupy the mind and this is one of them.

Out of Focus Projector

The first thing to do on entering the room is to check out the projector. The problem is the same as above. Little things can cause big problems.

External Noises

You are just asking for trouble if your meeting room is near the kitchen or the door to the kitchen. And who is meeting in the room next door? What if they have a jazz band for entertainment? Is the separation between rooms a solid wall or an accordion divider? If the meeting is at an airport hotel, guess what kind of noise you're going to be hearing? And don't wait until the day of the meeting to find out that your competitor is in the room next to yours.

External View

You might have a beautiful room, but what if it has picture windows overlooking the swimming pool? Worse, yet, what if they're having a fashion show on the deck of the pool or the swim suit contest for the local beauty queen? Don't think it can't happen to you.

Dos and Don'ts of Team Presentations

Sometimes nothing causes more conversation than who should be in on the presentation. Should we put all our chips on Wonder Woman, or should we bring an army?

Team presentations are to be avoided unless the specific situation dictates a team presentation. Team presentations are time-consuming, expensive, and—worst of all—usually mediocre at best. Believe me, it's difficult enough for a single presenter to plan, develop, and deliver an effective presentation without having to also conduct part-time musicians to sing the same song in the same key.

PROBLEMS OF TEAM PRESENTATIONS

1. Team presentations are notoriously difficult to develop. They are characterized by wasted effort, duplication, rework, last-minute changes, and missed assignments.

2. Team presentations require frequent meetings of highly paid people to develop the theme, the content, and the visuals. It's not uncommon to go through many iterations before agreement is reached on what the team is going to do. The more players there are, the longer it takes. Then we have the need for dry runs and dress rehearsals. All of this adds up to time and money.

3. A team presentation can backfire and cause you to lose the business. A team presentation gives your customer or client a first-hand preview of how well you and your people work together as a team. If your presentation looks more like the Marx Brothers than the Blue Angels, the customer or client may have serious reservations about your ability to manage a "big bucks" program, or successfully execute an important and multifaceted contract. By your own stumbling, fumbling, and uncoordinated presentation, you may have demonstrated, stronger than anything you could say, why the customer or client should give the business to someone else.

4. You can look and sound like different companies. The course of least resistance is to divide the presentation up into functional areas, and let each area or department do their own thing. And that's the problem. Everybody does their own thing, and that's what it looks like and sounds like. There is an absence of consistent strategy, focus, and closure on objectives. Might as well be three, four, or more different

companies. If further proof is needed, the visual aid media is often different, the design is different, the color scheme is different, the type of font is different, etc. It creates the impression that you've never met one another, let alone spoken to one another before the presentation.

5. Murphy's Law: Speaking from personal experience, I can tell you that there is plenty that can go wrong in a single presentation. To the extent that you use additional players, Murphy's Law becomes exponential and almost guarantees that your worst fears will become realities.

6. If you let the third team play, you will get what you deserve—a third-rate performance. Everybody may be famous for 15 minutes, but not in the way you expect. So let it not be on your stage, in front of your customer, at your expense.

7. Last-minute changes are a way of life when putting together presentations. The more important the presentation, the later and more numerous the changes. Your part may be as pure as Snow White, but getting seven dwarfs to rehearse a different tune at midnight is quite a trick.

8. What if there are troublemakers in the audience? They will want to be seen and heard for their expert knowledge, experience, and judgement. Often they will vocalize in areas that are either insignificant to the main issue, or so detailed or technical that they are incomprehensible to everybody else. Their objective may be to embarrass you and prove you wrong. Guess what happens? The presentation degenerates into a technical debate with the very few. Meanwhile, the key decision makers become disinterested, restless, and bored. The longer it goes, the worse it gets.

We have a suggested solution coming straight at you.

9. Finally, I would ask this acid test question. From the point of view of the audience, the customer, or the client, what are the benefits of parading your army across the stage? And from your point of view, if you want to win the game, wouldn't you rather have your number one hitter swinging the bat? Why settle for less than your best if you're playing in a high stakes game? After all, the messenger is often more important than the message.

The natural tendency of corporate America is to run presentations on the outside the way they do on the inside. The game plan on the inside is to let everybody who has a box on the organization chart play in the game—equal time for everybody and every department. After all, this is a democracy, and we don't play favorites, so everybody is entitled to a few minutes of glory. No wonder so many internal meetings are so boring. Have you ever heard a corporate economist?

A BETTER WAY

Is there a time and a place for team presentations? There sure is. Is there a better way to do them? There sure is.

If it's a big deal—if you've got a lot riding on the outcome, if there's a pot of gold for the winner—then listen up.

To get some answers let's ask some questions. For example, what is the rank and horsepower of the biggest decision maker in attendance? If you are short on titles or horsepower compared to Mr. or Ms. Big, then do everything you can to get the equivalent Mr./Ms. Big of your company, your bank, or your firm to come to the party. Their role is not to give the presentation but to balance the pedigree scales. The message they send by their presence says to the customer, client, or prospect, "Your business is important to me and my company."

This peer-to-peer presence is important to satisfy the unspoken protocol of business. It is absolutely critical to the success of your presentation if no one from your company or firm has ever met Mr./Ms. Big.

Next we ask, what functional departments will the customer or client have in the audience? The engineering department? The customer service department, the computer department, the company lawyer?

Just as important, we need to know in advance what their view is of their role in the meeting or presentation. Is it their role to listen and learn, or to question and interrogate?

If their view of their role is to listen and learn, then you are well advised to use your heaviest hitter for the entire presentation. You may well have some members of your army present to indicate by their presence their support, their commitment, and their personal interest in getting the business. But they are there for show, not to play. Let your Mr./Ms. Big introduce them and indicate the role each will play in delivering a value-added product or service. Although we expect the staff departments in the audience to listen and learn, there may be detailed or technical questions. If there are, you'll be glad you have your experts with you.

On the other hand, if we expect the various customer or client departments represented to have an active and participant role during the presentation, then we have a different ball game. Now we have to be prepared to deal with:

- The doubting Thomas
- The know-it-all
- The show-off
- The "I'm out to get you"
- The non-believer
- The adversary
- The devil's advocate
- And who knows what else

With these folks it's easy to get carried away with the technicalities of the battle, and forget that our purpose is to win the war.

One solution is to structure our presentation like this:

I.   Executive Summary

    Break

II. Implementation Plan

III. Training Support

    Break

IV. Engineering Considerations

V. Technical Support

    Break

VI. Data Processing Considerations

Now the very first thing we present is the structure of the presentation. We make it clear that the top decision makers who are not involved in the details may want to leave during the break at the end of the Executive Summary. We also make it clear that the technical details will be covered at their scheduled place in the presentation.

The objective here is to control the troublemakers and the nit-pickers during the critical Executive Summary to the key decision makers. We accomplish this by the way we structure the presentation and the breaks.

This has the further advantage of various user departments being able to schedule their time to attend only those modules of the presentation that pertain to them, i.e., the engineering department, the data processing department, etc.

It may not surprise you to learn that the troublemaker becomes less vocal and more subdued when the powers that be have left, and there's no one left to impress.

As for the team, we are now using our functional experts to talk to their counterparts in the audience. That's the best way to get the maximum mileage out of a team presentation.

Another advantage is that this structure makes it more likely that you will get the top decision makers to attend, since we have structured the Executive Summary just for them and made it convenient for them to leave when their part is over.

RULES OF THE ROAD FOR TEAM PRESENTATIONS

If your situation dictates a team presentation, here are some rules of the road to make it a winner.

1. Select a strong team leader with unquestioned leadership ability and the authority to make on-the-spot decisions about the content, delivery, and duration of each participant's presentation. The team leader does not necessarily have to be one of the presenters. Someone must assume overall responsibility for the structure, the content, the players, and the final result. You can't have a good performance of *A Chorus Line* without a strong director.

2. Follow the bouncing ball of the Presentation Planning Guide in Chapter 16. It's your best assurance of having a successful presentation.

3. Dedicate a wall in a "war room," conference room, or office to a "storyboard." What is a storyboard? It is a layout in hand-drawn rough form of each visual aid for the presentation on 8½ x 11 sheets stuck on a wall with masking tape. It will have the title or heading for the visual, a rough hand-drawn sketch of any graph, chart, or other graphics, and bullets for the main points to be made.

Don't be fooled by the simplicity of the concept of a storyboard. It is critical to the success of a team presentation.

A. It allows all the players and management to review and analyze the organization, the flow, the transition between presenters, and the consistency of the content in accomplishing the objectives of the presentation.

B. Redundancies, inconsistencies, irrelevant material, and missing key points, examples, and references are easily identified.

C. It is quick and easy to make changes before the costly and time-consuming steps of artwork and visual aid production begin.

D. Storyboards are easier to follow than outlines or narratives. They also give the participants and reviewers an actual picture of what the audience will see.

E. A storyboard gives an early indication of the duration of a presentation. Business or technical visuals typically take 30 seconds to two minutes per visual to cover. For technical presentations, one to one and a half minutes per visual is a good target. So if you have time constraints you can get an early picture of where you stand, and how much might need to be cut.

4. Be sure the visuals for each presenter use a consistent format, color scheme, and type style so the total result is perceived as a well-coordinated, single presentation.

5. Take the time to develop a logical and smooth transition between presenters. It's the difference between a bunch of amateurs and true professionals.

6. If it's important to rehearse for a one-man show, it's absolutely critical for a marching band. I don't mean a "walk-through" but a full dress rehearsal of the real thing. Success is spelled R-E-H-E-A-R-S-E.

If you want to see an example of a good team presentation in living color, watch the six o'clock news. Note the coordination, the flow, and the transitions between the anchor, the on-site special reporter, the weather person, the traffic report, and the sports summary.

We can learn another important lesson from the six o'clock news. The players are selected for their communication skills—not for their knowledge of the subject.

WHAT IF YOU'RE SELLING A BODY

There are other considerations if you're in advertising, banking, accounting, consulting, the stock market, service industries in general, or if you're selling the concept of an "account executive." In these cases you may think you're selling a service, but the client is more likely to view it as their buying the talent or experience of an individual. From the customer's or client's point of view, the quality of the service or support is more likely to be seen as a function of the individual than it is of the company.

This is also true of many product companies, especially if they have a heavy support and service component. In the computer business, for example, we find that the single biggest variable in the level of customer satisfaction is the marketing rep assigned to the account.

If you're playing in this arena then the person you're selling should be the star of the show. The organization and delivery of the presentation should be built around your "star." Others may participate, but your "star" must appear to be the leader of the band. The presentation should be structured to highlight his or her talents, experience, and competence.

By words and deeds, the Mr. or Ms. Big of your organization needs to convey confidence and respect for the "star." Further, if the customer or client is, in effect, buying an individual, they should perceive that the purpose of the organization is to support the individual assigned to their account. This can be demonstrated by a presentation of the talent, resources, and specialists that the "star" has at her command. It's even better if you can demonstrate what a great quarterback the "star" is by examples and references.

Customers and clients want to believe that they are being serviced by the best—the most talented, the most experienced, and the smartest. If you can fill in those blanks, focus on building a personal relationship (remember Aristotle), and give a professional presentation, you will win the game.

The bottom line of the marketplace is this. If you're a fish in a small pond and not in the Fortune 500, don't despair. The Davids of this world, with the right talent and chemistry, are beating Goliaths every day. You can be one of them.

GETTING
THEM BACK
FROM THE
BREAK

If there is any bigger problem than getting them back from the break, I don't know what it is. If your scheduled 15-minute break turns into 30 minutes, and you have two breaks in the morning and two in the afternoon, you have lost an hour of time on your program.

Before we talk about solving that problem, let's talk about the frequency of breaks. How long should we go before we take a break? The best answer comes from audience sensitivity and common sense. We should never go for two hours without a break. On the other hand, if you take a break in less than an hour you are not making efficient use of time. The right answer lies somewhere in between. It's far better to err on the side of being too soon rather than too late.

Breaks should be planned in conjunction with the duration of a presentation. For example, suppose your presentation takes 1 hour and 45 minutes. Should you take a break after 45 minutes? I think not. A better plan is to identify a specific place in the presentation where you could have the audience take a stand-up stretch while you continue the presentation. A good place to do this is where you tell a joke, a story, or a personal experience, or so forth. For example, you might say, "Let me tell you a personal experience that illustrates the point we're talking about. While I do, why don't we all stand up and stretch our legs?" That's smooth, flows well, and seems to be naturally built into the presentation. Don't forget to invite them to sit back down at the end of your story.

Let's take another example. Suppose you have a 30-minute presentation that follows a 45-minute presentation with no break in between. Even though the elapsed time is only 1 hour, 15 minutes, you will be well advised to ask the audience to take an in-place 60-second stretch before you start the second presentation.

That will wake them up, get the juices flowing, and psychologically reset the audience to zero in preparation for the next presentation. You need to force a mental break from the first presentation. A stand-up stretch will help to do that. The absolutely worst way to have a break is to be motoring through your presentation, look down at your watch, and suddenly announce, "I didn't realize what time it is—would you like to take a break?" On the contrary, breaks need to be planned and built into your program at specific and strategic points.

The next rule is to have everybody on the same time. If there is a clock on the wall, use it. If there is no wall clock, ask them to use your time, and tell them what it is.

The break is not a stand-alone event. If the presentation should have started at 9:00, and you started ten minutes late, that sends a message to the audience that you will probably start late after the break. You pay the price in more ways than one if you don't start on time.

On the other hand, if you started your presentation on time, then you have signaled the audience that you will also start on time after the break.

DON'T SAY "LET'S TAKE A TEN-MINUTE BREAK"

Don't announce a break the way most people do. Don't say, "Let's take a ten-minute break." Here's the problem. The people are out in the hall, drinking coffee, in the rest room, or on the phone. Question. When did the ten minutes start? Answer. Nobody knows. How are you going to know when to come back if you don't know when you started. The solution is *not* to announce the *duration* of the break, but the *return time* after the break. So we would say, "Let's take a break and return at 10:30." A good technique is to also write the return time on a flip chart as you say it.

ANTICIPATE THEIR NEEDS

Another technique for getting them back from the break is to anticipate their needs and requirements. For example, many people head for the phones at the break. They want to call in, check in, and see if there are any fires burning back at the ranch. Well, there is no way you can take a 10-minute break and get them back from the phones. So you might think the answer is to take a longer break. Possibly, but there is a better answer. If the meeting lasts a half-day, you can announce up front that there will be a 10-minute break and a 20-minute break. You further state that the intent of the long break is to give the attendees time to call the office. That way, the total break time is no greater than if you had two 15-minute breaks, but the breaks are better planned to meet the needs of the audience.

GIVE THEM THE BALL

Another technique for getting them back from the break is to get their agreement on how long the break should be. Here's the way this works. When you come to the place in the presentation where you have planned the break, you announce to the group that you are going to take a break. You would then state that this is their meeting and ask them how long a break they want. You might prompt them by saying, "Ten minutes?" "Fifteen minutes?" Someone will volunteer a number like "Ten minutes." You then ask the audience, "Is ten minutes all right? Does anybody have a problem with ten minutes?" If there is no response you can announce the time the meeting will resume (ten minutes later).

What has happened here is that you have established a psychological gentlemen's agreement. Since no one objected to the ten minutes, and you gave them the opportunity to do just that, your audience will tend to feel obliged to be back on time.

IT'S SHOWTIME

Another technique is to do what they do at the theater, the opera, and the symphony. During the intermission, blink the house lights and the hall lights off and on to announce that the show is about to begin.

PREVIEW OF COMING ATTRACTIONS

Millions of people schedule their entire day around the TV soap operas. How do the networks get people to do that? They do it by giving the audience a compelling reason to tune back in. Just before the break (yesterday) they built up to an emotional event, a crisis, a cliff hanger. "Tune in tomorrow and find out—is Susie really _____ _____ _____?" We can do the same thing in our own way. Plan and schedule the break so that you can say something like, "When we return from the break at 10:30, we will talk about the Seven Deadly Sins (or how to make $10,000 more money every year, or a secret that is 4,000 years old, or Hot Drugs for Sweaty Palms)." Well, you get the idea.

TURN THE LIGHTS OUT

Or you can play dirty pool and show a short movie right after the break. That gives you an excuse to close the doors and keep them closed. Anyone who does try to get in is faced with a pitch black room, must stumble over people, and may end up sitting in somebody's lap. Next time they'll be on time.

KEEP THE DOORS CLOSED

Continuing with the psychological warfare strategy, there is another thing you can do at the start of the meeting that sends a powerful message to the audience. The message you send is, "This is a business meeting and it's going to be run like a business meeting." The way you send that message is to keep the meeting room doors closed until the exact time the meeting is to start. Then you open the doors and let the audience in. Many people have never experienced that, but they sure understand the message.

SING A SONG OR TELL A JOKE

Here's a trick that works wonders. When you announce the break and the restart time of 10:30, just add that they can come back anytime they want to, but if it's after 10:30 they have to either sing a song or tell a joke.

A final tip on breaks is to make a visual aid that shows the location of the restrooms, phones, coffee, and so on. This will save both you and them time and questions. In the design of the visual aid you can leave space to write in the restart time. They will be impressed with your foresight, planning, and thoughtfulness.

Time Control

The great enemy of all meetings, conferences, seminars, and presentations is time. How many meetings have you ever attended that finished early?

Here's the kind of thing that happens. The meeting starts ten minutes late. The introductions take 15 minutes instead of five. The welcome takes 15 instead of ten. The first speaker takes 50 minutes instead of the 35 he was scheduled for. The first coffee break lasts 20 minutes instead of ten, and so on.

You are scheduled to be on the program at 4:00. Well, by that time the meeting is more than an hour behind schedule and there's another speaker ahead of you who has not yet been introduced.

That brings us to Rule #1: Get on the program early in the day. Not only is the audience fresher, more attentive, and more interested—you also avoid all the things that can go wrong during the day.

Rule #2 is: Don't contribute to the problem. An inexperienced presenter will almost always run over time. A good presenter will finish on time. A better presenter will finish five minutes early. Within reasonable limits a better presenter can finish when he or she wants to finish. How?

First let's talk about what tends to happen to the inexperienced presenter who is not well-prepared and has not rehearsed.

About 45 minutes into an allotted one hour, the inexperienced presenter finally notices what time it is, realizes there is only 15 minutes left, and that he or she isn't even halfway through the presentation. The instinctive reaction is to rush through the remaining material and set a new world's record for words-per-minute.

Rushing is worse than ineffective. It causes an adverse reaction. The audience becomes uncomfortable with the rush, the pace, and the rapid-fire words. Additionally, the close—which is the most important part of the presentation—is rushed through and completely loses its impact and effectiveness. The presenter has become his or her own worst enemy. Rushing is self-defeating. People will remember not what was said but *how long* it took to say it.

The better presenter will have anticipated the requirement for time control. As part of the planning and construction of the presentation, he or she will have created a *modular outline* of the key elements of the presentation. In Figure 14A we see an example of how that might look.

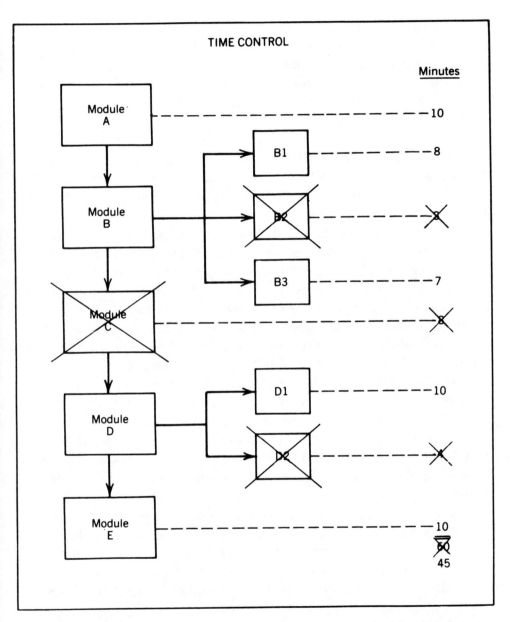

FIGURE 14A We can control the time of a presentation by deciding in advance the priority of things to delete.

This particular presentation is made up of five logical components: A, B, C, D, and E. Think of these as minichapters. Two of them (B and D) are further broken down into subheadings within a chapter.

The second step for the better presenter comes as a by-product of rehearsing. A record is made of the time it takes to complete each component of the presentation.

The third and final step is to evaluate the relative value and contribution of each component to achieving the final object, then answer the following question: "If I wanted to reduce my total time by 10 or 15 minutes, what elements would I eliminate, and what would their priorities be?"

In Figure 14A we see that the presenter would eliminate B2, C, and D2. That reduces a one-hour presentation to 45 minutes. The key point is that the presenter has gone through this entire thought process in advance. Thus, when the presenter has a need to cut it short, he or she already knows—in order of priority—what to eliminate.

We never want to rush through a presentation. Instead, our solution to time constraints is to eliminate elements of the presentation. The audience will never know that anything was eliminated.

You will find this difficult to do if you are the person who created the presentation. The pride of ownership and authorship will compel you to think that you have to present it all. But my experience is that the 45-minute presentation goes just as well as the full one-hour version. In fact, I suspect that you will find as I have, that a shorter version often goes better than the longer version. People remember more if you tell them less.

Using this technique, I suggest you complete your presentation five minutes early. What a breath of fresh air you will be to your audience. Rarely in the course of a million presentations has anyone finished early. You can be one in a million. And if you're in the marketing game, you will have differentiated yourself from your competitor. It's almost a sure bet that your competitor will run over.

Now that we know how to control time, it's important to build in a check point periodically during the presentation. The checkpoint will tell us if we are ahead of schedule or behind schedule.

The way we do this is to figure out in advance exactly where we should be after 15 minutes into the presentation. We then write on our

cheat sheet, "TC + 15." This means, "Time check for 15 min.
to this point." So if we started at 9:00 A.M. when we get to th.
sheet it should be 9:15. If it's 9:20 then we know we are five mi..
behind schedule, and we need to eliminate one of the preplann.
elements and make up time. We do the same thing for 30 minutes into
the presentation (TC + 30), and for 45 minutes (TC + 45).

You need to know that you will always start at least five minutes
later than you think, even if you start on time. Let me explain.

If the program says you start at 9:00, you don't. Even if the audience
are in their seats at 9:00, there's always an announcement or two, a
question or two, your introduction, and so forth. Then you have to get
to the front. By the time you say your first word it will be at least 9:05.

So even though the program says you have an hour (9:00-10:00), we
want to plan our presentation for 50 minutes. We lose five minutes on
the front end, and we want to finish five minutes early.

The bottom line is that an hour on the schedule really means a 50-
minute presentation. If you want or need one hour, ask for one hour
and ten minutes on the schedule.

The worst thing a presenter can do is to be dull, dry, and boring. The
second worst thing a presenter can do is run overtime. If you follow
these techniques, you can finish when you choose to finish.

TIP #1   The Rule of 60 Percent

Only 60 percent will show up. So set up chairs for only 60 percent of the number you think will come. Keep some extra chairs nearby but out of sight.

When the 60 percent show up it will look like a packed house. If more show up, you can easily get the extra chairs for what is obviously an overflow crowd. Whatever happens, you have a full house. That's heads you win, tails you win.

But before you count your winnings, check out Tip #2.

TIP #2   Don't Be Alone in This Wicked World

That's what the people will feel like if you have a meeting for ten in a room designed for 50. The room size is very important. It must be appropriate to the size of the group. Not too big, not too small, but just right.

TIP #3   You Can Be Special

There's no rule that says you have to provide a handout at the end. But you will be special if you do. People like getting something extra and free. Just a one-page summary will do the trick. Even better would be reprints of articles, a list of resources or numbers to call, a bibliography, or a roster of attendees. Be sure to include your card, and your network will grow and grow.

TIP #4   If It Ain't Right, It Ain't Right

If someone's name gets misspelled on their badge or place card they will say it's okay—it's no big deal—it happens all the time. *Don't you believe it.* It's not okay and it is a big deal, so fix it now—right now. Have some blank badges and place cards ready and waiting.

TIP #5   Always Start and End with the Lights Fully Bright

The opening and the close are the most important parts of the presentation. Be sure all projectors are off and the lights fully bright so the focus is on you for the opening and the close.

TIP #6   High Tech Without Moving Parts

If the number one high tech invention of the decade is the TV "clicker," then second place goes to the portable and wireless microphone that clips on to your tie or lapel. It gives you freedom from the podium, keeps you from falling on your face by tripping over cords, and lets you speak in a more normal and natural voice. It's even effective for small groups if you're competing with a high noise level of the heating and air conditioning system, or with the folks next door.

TIP #7   How To Minimize the Mumbling, Whispering, and Cliques

You can control the seating by printing and positioning the place cards or tent cards in advance. Separate the folks who work together or play together. And position the females between two males. Both will like it better. And, I guarantee you, there will be less talking.

TIP #8   Don't Bend Over—Stand Straight

You'll be bending and bowing to change transparencies and read your cheat sheets if you are using overheads. You can stand straight and look professional if you ask, "Where's the copier room?" What you want is the bottom of an empty box that copier paper comes in. Turn it upside down beside the overhead projector, and you have a raised platform that's exactly even with the top of the projector. Works like a charm.

TIP #9   If You Go Back—You'll Get Lost

If you try to go back to find a previously used visual so you can refer to it a second time, it will be impossible to find. It will have disappeared. A better answer is to make multiple copies of a visual if you plan to use it multiple times.

TIP #10   If You're the Last To Go, There Won't Be a Line

Don't head for the rest room at the start of a break. There will be a line and you'll waste your time. Hang around in the meeting room. Some folks from your audience will want to talk with you—some will have questions. This is an excellent opportunity to get feedback on how it's going. It's also a good time to talk privately with any troublemakers .
   Speaking of trouble—see Tip #10A.

TIP #10A   Nothing Is Ever as Simple as It Sounds

Take the coffee break, for example. A lot of people don't like coffee. They want decaffeinated or tea. Of the tea drinkers, some want sugar, and some want lemon. Of the sugar users some want regular, and some want low-cal. Have alternates available.
   And there can be more trouble at the coffee break. Tip #10B tells you how.

TIP #10B Don't Have a Traffic Jam at the Coffee Pot

You will if you don't have the right sequence. Place the cups *before* the coffee, not after. And put the cream and sugar and other supplies on a table separate from the coffee. That will relieve congestion and smooth the flow.

TIP #11 How to Have Your Cake and Eat It, Too—Or How to Start on Time Without Starting on Time

Start the meeting on time with a three-to-five-minute slide show of famous, interesting, humorous, and provocative quotes. That gives the audience another three to five minutes to assemble and settle down before the main event. (And you *did* start on time.)

TIP #12 You Can Leave Your Bow at Home, But Bring Your Own Arrows

Signs with arrows pointing in the direction of your meeting will be appreciated by your audience. But not just any sign. First impressions count. Signs with your company name and logo that are professional in appearance will always create a good first impression.

That's a very different impression from signs made at the last minute from a few words and an arrow scrawled in pen on loose-leaf paper.

TIP #13 Some See from the Front, Some See from the Back—If You Do It Twice You'll Get Both Right

It's common to have place cards or tent cards so we'll know who's who. Too often the name is on the front only. If you will put it on both sides, you will make everybody happy. That allows the ones in the back to also see who's who.

TIP #14 How to Make a Pointer in Ten Seconds with Four Rubber Bands

If you travel with your presentation, what are you going to do for a pointer? One answer is the little metal gadget about the size of a tire gauge that telescopes out like a radio aerial to make a pointer. I guess they're all right. I just never trusted anybody that used one. In addition, if you are the least bit nervous, the slightest quiver of your fingers will be amplified by a factor of ten. So instead of having a slight quiver in the hand it will look like you have Saint Vitus' dance by the time it gets to the end of the pointer.

A better solution is to make your own pointer on the spot. Tear off three blank pages of flip-chart paper, roll them up very tight, and distribute four rubber bands up and down the shaft. Makes a perfect pointer without the Saint Vitus' dance. If you have another few seconds you can take a Magic Marker and color the pointer blue.

Note: Do not color the six inches at the bottom where you grip the pointer. If you do, you'll end up with a blue hand.

TIP #15   Need a Room? Call the Bank

Many banks and savings and loans have community meeting rooms. More often than not, they're free. Also available are meeting rooms at the main public library, and even at some branches of the public library. Other possibilities for finding meeting rooms are lodges and fraternal organizations, shopping centers, and auditoriums at private schools.

TIP #16   Don't Dot the I's and Cross the T's

Round off those big numbers. The detail will only confuse and make it hard to remember. So $501,247.00 becomes $500,000, and $998,482.00 becomes a million dollars. Don't mess around with odd-lots.

TIP #17   When to Use What

Use graphs for sales figures, financial time series, or any set of numbers for which you want to show the trend over a period of time. No more than two or three lines on a graph, please.

If you have to show a complicated graph with many lines, use transparent overlays. That makes it easy for the audience to follow one thing at a time, and you get the benefit of a better understood composite chart when you finish.

Use pie charts to show the distribution of a whole into its component parts. Examples are: budgets, market share, income sources, expense analysis, and so forth. No more than eight or ten divisions please. Lump small ones together and call them miscellaneous.

Use bar charts to represent quantity by the length (if horizontal) or height (if vertical). These are also effective when used in conjunction with color coding to show comparisons, such as this year versus last year. Use tables to show things like a mileage/distance chart or timetables. Circle several examples to talk about that illustrate your point.

TIP #18   If You're Out of Date, You're Out to Lunch

Nothing will destroy your credibility quicker than to use out-of-date facts and figures. And for heaven's sake, don't apologize for obsolete numbers. Get them current, and do it now. Sorry about those harsh words—but this is important.

TIP #19   Let's Do It in Living Color

Most presentations are done in black and white. How drab, dreary, and depressing can you get? Hollywood learned a better way sixty years ago. Add life and excitement to your presentation by doing it in color. After all, does it take any longer to do it in color? Of course not. Does it cost any more? Maybe a dime or a dollar.

Again, the quality of your presentation is a mirror image of the quality of your firm, your product, your service, your support, and you. So make yourself a breed apart. Be first class by going first class with color.

There are two problems with color. The first one is covered in Tip #19A.

TIP #19A   A Rainbow Is Pretty in the Sky But Not on the Screen

Six or eight colors on a single flip, foil, or slide is too much of a good thing. So limit your colors to two or three. But look out for Tip #19B.

TIP #19B   Some Are Better Than Others—Colors, That Is

Choose your colors carefully. Some colors are difficult to see from the back of the room. For example, colors like pink, orange, and yellow are no-nos—they just don't show up well.

The final tip on color is subtle, but has the impact of a sledge hammer. Straight ahead to 20.

TIP #20   Red Stands for Stop, Danger, and Blood

After all, stop signs are red, fire trucks are red, high voltage signs are red. So when you show a slide, a transparency, or write on a flip chart, do it in red to indicate danger, a problem, or the competition. Color coding can complement and enhance the point you are making.

TIP #21   There Is No Substitute for the Real Thing

A 30-second demonstration is more effective than 30 minutes of words. The best method of proving a point, validating a theory, or convincing the skeptic is a demonstration.

If you would like to have a lot of fun, pretend you have never seen a cigarette. Then have someone hand you an unopened pack and ask them to explain to you *with words only* how to open the pack, extract a cigarette, put the right end in the mouth, light it, and smoke.

TIP #22   Should I Go First or Last?

Go first. They will be more interested and pay more attention. And if you have read this book you will have set the bar so high that you become the standard against which others are measured. If you go last they will be tired out, worn out, and behind schedule.

TIP #23   A Minute Is Too Long But a Millisecond Is Just Right

As soon as you show a new slide or transparency, allow a millisecond or two for the visual impact to sink in. Then explain in general terms what the graph or chart is going to show, any assumptions that are made, and an explanation of the X and Y axes.

TIP #24   You Can Spot the Difference Between an Amateur and a Professional Before You See The First Slide

When the amateur turns the projector on, the audience is hit with a glaring bright light that fills the screen. The same thing happens to the amateur after the last slide. The professional eliminates the glaring light by putting a blank, opaque slide at the beginning and end of the presentation.

TIP #25   The Presenter's First-Aid Kit, Or Don't Get Caught with Your Lights Out

You only need one item in your first-aid kit—a spare bulb. The day will come when it will save your life. Well, maybe not your life, but at the time it will sure seem like it.

TIP #26   Don't Get Caught Saying, "Next Slide, Please"

If a football coach can run an entire game from the sidelines using visual signals, surely to goodness you can work out one visual signal to tell your associate when to change slides or transparencies.

TIP #27   Let the Spotlights Help You—Not Hurt You

Many of the rooms you will be in will have recessed spotlights in the ceiling. Be sure to position your screen to keep the spotlights off the screen. But position your flip-chart stand to have a spotlight on it. Careful now, a few inches can make a big difference. That roll at the top of a flip chart projects out slightly and can cast a shadow half way down the flip chart. If you move it six inches you can solve the problem.

TIP #28   Never, Never, Never Pack and Ship Your Presentation

The only thing worse than being up the creek without a paddle is being at the meeting without your presentation. That's what will happen to

'I lost a fortune in the stock market today . . . yours.'

FIGURE 15A Keep your eyes open for cartoons to illustrate your points. They add spice to the presentation.

you if you pack your presentation in your luggage and check it at the airport. That's the time your luggage will get lost. There is only one answer. Always hand-carry your presentation.

TIP #29 Everybody Loves Cartoons

So keep your eyes open for cartoons that you can use in your presentation to highlight and emphasize a point. They will add a little spice or at least some salt and pepper to your presentation.

TIP #30 KISS—"Keep It Simple, Stupid"

Complex charts or graphs that make multiple points at the same time may be clever to create, but they are confusing to your audience.

And watch those complex words. See Tip #30A.

TIP #30A KISS—Version #2

Don't use technical words, industry language, or phrases and acronyms that would not be well known to your audience. If any are central to your presentation, use them, but be sure you define them first.

TIP #31 Never Play with a Full Deck

Never walk in a room in full view of the audience with an armload of two or three hours' worth of material. Worse still is stacking the entire presentation on a table in the front of the room. If you do, the audience will be preoccupied with the size of the stack and how much longer is left to go. "What do you think, Joe?" "Looks to me like another two or three hours."

When you arrive early, what you want to do is hide all of the presentation material except for enough material to carry you to the first break.

FIGURE 15B Simple circles and arrows can enhance your message.

TIP #32   Use the Magic of the Circle

If you have a lot of transparencies, or slides with a lot of words, you can make them more interesting and more readable by breaking them up. The use of simple circles, rectangles, arrows, and so on can enhance the appearance and the interest of words.

TIP #33   50 Percent of the Time You Don't Need a Screen

All you need is a light-colored wall to project on. Just set the pictures that are hanging on the wall down on the floor and you're in business.

TIP #34   A Portable Emergency Screen

The only problem with projecting on a wall is that sometimes there will be wallpaper with a design—like red roses. You can't project on red-rose wallpaper.

That's where the emergency kit comes in. The emergency kit consists of four pieces of blank flip-chart paper and a roll of masking tape. It will only take about 20 seconds to tape in place a temporary screen of flip-chart

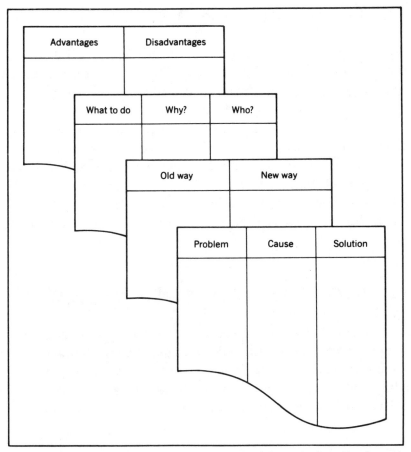

FIGURE 15C A structured format will keep the mind on the target.

paper. Always use masking tape, never Scotch tape. The red roses will come off with the Scotch tape and you will have to pay for repapering a wall.

TIP #35   How to Keep Their Eyes on The Target—And on You, Too

You can control the audience by establishing a format on a flip chart or chalkboard for the presentation and the discussion.

A structured format will keep the mind of the audience on the target, save time, and help you accomplish your objective.

Check out Figure 15C and see what you think.

TIP #36   Don't Get Caught in the Dark

If it hasn't happened to you yet, it's just a matter of time. Just as you get into your presentation, the lights go out. That's not a malfunction. Some misguided good samaritan has turned the lights out, thinking they are doing you a favor. They come from the old school that says any time you project anything on a screen—turn the lights out. They don't realize that modern overhead projections are designed to be seen with the lights on, and that you want them on so you can have eye contact and group participation.

So before you start, check out the location of the light switches so you can have light on the audience, light on the subject, and light on yourself.

TIP #37   He Can Sell Your Product Better Than You Can

The person who can sell your product better than you can yourself is the satisfied user. So plan at a strategic point in the presentation to call on a satisfied user to give a testimonial. Two or three would be even better.

If they can't be there, play a tape cassette of their testimonials. If you don't have that, show pictures of them and give their testimonials for them.

TIP #38   Give Them Something to Look at Before the Show Starts

Have something showing on the screen when they walk in.

- A pretty picture
- A welcome
- A provocative quote
- If they're all from the same company, have the company name and their logo
- The title page of your presentation (see Figure 15D)

FIGURE 15D Have something showing on the screen when they walk in—like the title page of your presentation.

TIP #39   Whom Should I Follow?

Answer: An economist. The only exception is the one who won the Nobel Prize. If you can't follow an economist, then try to follow anyone who has a Ph.D. It's 20 to 1 that they will be dull, dry, and boring.

TIP #40   Emily Post Says, "Don't Point"

You shouldn't, either. So avoid that tendency to point when you want to call on someone. Instead, extend your hand, fingers together and palm up. And please, don't ever point to someone with a pointer.

TIP #41   If You Tend to Scream and Shout. . . .

Remember these words of wisdom: "People will believe anything if you whisper it."

TIP #42 It's Okay to Ship Your Handouts If . . .

. . . you hand carry an original copy with you. Then if things go wrong and your handouts get lost, a fast copy center can put you back in business.

TIP #43   Don't Let the Holes Show Through

If you use a sheet of three-ring binder paper for the revelation technique, the holes will show on the screen. It looks really tacky. A better choice is blank copier paper with no holes. This can also serve double duty by being your cheat sheet.

TIP #44   A Tilt Forward Will Make It Straight

When you project up to a large screen the projected image is wider at the top of the screen than it is at the bottom. Some people refer to this as the keystone effect.

The solution is to tilt the top of the screen forward. That will square it up perpendicular to the projected light. Some screens are designed to do that. Check the supporting framework of the screen.

If it looks different from any you've ever seen, then I betcha it will tilt at the top. Sometimes screens that pull down from the ceiling are designed to push back at the bottom and fasten to the wall—the result is the same.

TIP #45   Make Another One-Time Decision

Are you going to stand to the right or to the left of the overhead projector? Don't mix it up. Make a one-time decision and always stand on that side. You'll be more comfortable if you do.

FYI, most right-handed people feel more comfortable standing to the left of the projector as they face it.

While we're making decisions, go on to Tip #45A.

TIP #45A   Make Another One-Time Decision

When you lay your transparencies beside the projector, are you going to turn them from left to right or from right to left? Make a one-time decision and do it the same way every time. If you don't, the time will come when you forget where you are and what comes next. This is the same as hitting the backward button of the slide projector instead of the forward. By the way, you can solve *that* problem by taping the hand-held control gadget to the top of the table so that the forward button is always toward you.

TIP #46   Turn It Off When Not in Use

The projector, that is. Here's the problem. The human eye is naturally drawn toward bright light. If you leave the projector on when you are not using it, the eyes will be drawn to the light, and the ears will be drawn to your voice. The eyes will win and the ears will lose. You can solve the problem by eliminating the contention. Just turn off the projector.

TIP #47   Do Your Filing on Your Own Time—Not the Audience's Time

Have you ever seen this? The presenter walks to the front with a three-ring binder containing her transparencies. She pops open the binder, removes and shows the first transparency. Now comes the problem. She attempts to refile the transparency in the binder with one hand. It seems like it takes forever. I think the audience can legitimately say, "Do your filing on your own time, not on our time."

TIP #48   Use Your Pen For a Pointer

If you have a large audience and a large screen, a standard pointer won't reach the full screen. The solution is to use your pen directly on the transparency itself. Don't try to hold it in midair—it will quiver and shake. Drop the pen on the transparency, move the point to where you want it, then remove your hand.

As a by-product, this technique allows you to always be facing the audience, not the screen.

TIP #49   What's Hard with One Can Be Easy with Two

Overhead projectors, that is. This allows you to have the big picture on one projector while you review and show the component parts on the second. That way you can show the forest and the trees at the same time. Very good for complex subjects.

TIP #50   How to Separate the Few from the Many

If you end up with a transparency full of numbers, use a felt-tip pen to circle the few you want to talk about. If you use different colored pens to circle numbers, you can refer to them by color. Sure makes it a lot easier to follow.

TIP #51   How to Make Black and White Look Like a Sunrise

If you are handed a canned pitch with black and white transparencies, you can change them to beautiful color in two seconds. You do this by overlaying the black and white transparencies with a blank colored transparency. Just three or four different colored blank transparencies can make the presentation look like a sunrise.

TIP #52   If You Can Read It on the Floor, You've Got It Just Right

Is the lettering on your transparencies too small to be seen from the back of the room? Place a transparency on the floor. If you can read it while standing up, it's probably large enough.

TIP #53   A Rubber Band Will Keep the Flips Off the Floor

A common design of flip-chart stands is to have two metal posts that correspond to the holes in your flip-chart paper. Trouble is, when you turn the pages the paper has a tendency to buckle in the middle or fall off one or both of the metal posts. A simple solution is to loop two rubber bands together and stretch them across both metal posts. One won't reach across, but two will do the job.

TIP #54   How to Preserve, Protect, and Defend Your Flip Charts

One of the problems with flip charts is that they tend to get beaten up and dog-eared, especially if you travel with them. You can triple their life span with a little tender loving care. Here's how.

Get a cardboard tube to carry them in. (The kind with a plastic lid that fits on both ends.) You want the tube to be slightly longer than your flip charts are wide. An excess of about one inch on each end will be fine. You can get these tubes at an art supply or office supply store—or check your own mail room.

Now lay your flip charts on the floor face down on top of two or three sheets of blank paper. Position the blank sheets so that they are slightly off square to your presentation flip charts. Now roll them up to fit into the tube. Please note that if the blank sheets are slightly off square, there will be excess paper hanging over each end when you roll it up. But the excess paper will be the blank paper. Note also that you are rolling up your presentation backward. This will eliminate the curling up at the bottom when you put them on a flip-chart stand.

Now we Scotch tape one of the plastic lids in place. We wad up two or three pieces of paper towels and drop them down the tube. Slide the rolled-up presentation into the tube on top of the wadded-up paper towels. Place more wadded-up paper towels in the open end and Scotch tape the other plastic lid in place. That's it. You now have your presentation safe and secure for travel.

TIP #55   An Accident Waiting to Happen

Sooner or later you are going to be walking up to give a presentation and drop the whole show on the floor. It's bad enough picking up your foils, but the really bad news is that they are now out of sequence and you don't remember for sure what went where.

The first-aid for this kind of disaster is to be sure you have numbered the material sequentially so you can easily reassemble it. And speaking of disaster, make an extra copy of your presentation and keep it locked away somewhere. Some day you'll be glad you did.

TIP #56   Don't Fiddle and Fumble with the Flip Charts

Have you ever seen the next speaker trying to get their flip charts threaded on the metal post? Two or three fit on one side while two or three are dropping off the other. What a mess. Seems like it takes forever. That will make a nervous wreck out of anybody.

You can solve this problem in advance by having your flip charts held together with two of the large paper-clip-type clamps at the top. The holes are prealigned and the entire unit (clamps intact) is slipped over the metal post.

TIP #57   How to Preserve, Protect, and Defend Your Transparencies

You can do this by inserting them in the standard three-ring binder acetate protective folder. They still project just fine.

TIP #58   Would You Hang a Picture Without a Frame?

Then don't show a transparency without a frame. You can make a frame on the top of the overhead projector by using a strip of masking tape on the left and right to block out the excess light.

TIP #59   How to Find One Among Many

If you are drawing charts as you go, or are using them as your alternate medium, you might want to refer back to a particular chart. That's a technique of relating a future point to a past principle. It ties the presentation together and makes the conclusions more acceptable since the logic is better established.

The problem is, how do you find the page you want to turn back to?

Here's the answer. When you are explaining the chart the first time just turn the corner down before you turn the chart over, just like you would the page of a book. Then when you want to find that chart, turn all the charts back over to their original positions. The one with the corner turned down will stand out.

TIP #60   Start with a Clean Slate

You can do this by cleaning the top of the overhead projector. Here's the deal.

I promise you, every overhead projector you walk up to will be dirty. The top of the glass will project fingerprints, lint, smudge marks, spilled coffee, and who knows what.

Here's the solution. Since you will have to go to the bathroom many times before the presentation anyway, just bring back some paper towels the next trip. Five dry ones in one hand, and five soggy, wet ones in the other. Then clean the top of the glass just like it was the windshield of your car.

The nonverbal communication says, "I'm a professional and this is a quality show—you deserve the best." (At the very least, a clean slate.)

Next thing you know, your colleagues will start cleaning their slates too. Quality is contagious. Pass it on.

Presentation Planning Guide

Let me tell you a secret. It took me ten years to learn this.

<u>**95% of How Well Your Presentation is Going to Go Is Determined Before You Even Start.**</u>

The following steps, if followed in sequence, will guarantee a winning presentation every time.

Steps To A Winning Presentation

DEFINE OBJECTIVES — What is the purpose of the presentation? When it's all over—what is it that you want the audience to do?

DESIGN CLOSE — This is the most important part of the presentation. Play your best cards here. Sing your best song last.

CREATE OPENING — This is the second most important part of the presentation. A set-up for the close and a first impression of you.

OUTLINE BODY — What is your story? Support your case with reasons, facts, proof, examples, references, etc.

ADD SPICE — How do I get the audience's attention and keep their interest?

DESIGN VISUAL AIDS — You are 43% more likely to persuade, and you can charge 26% more money using visual aids.

TAILOR TO AUDIENCE — Convey the perception that your presentation was created just for them.

CREATE CHEAT SHEETS — Here are your wake-up calls. This is what you say next.

REHEARSE — **There is no fast food-line. You have to pay your dues.**

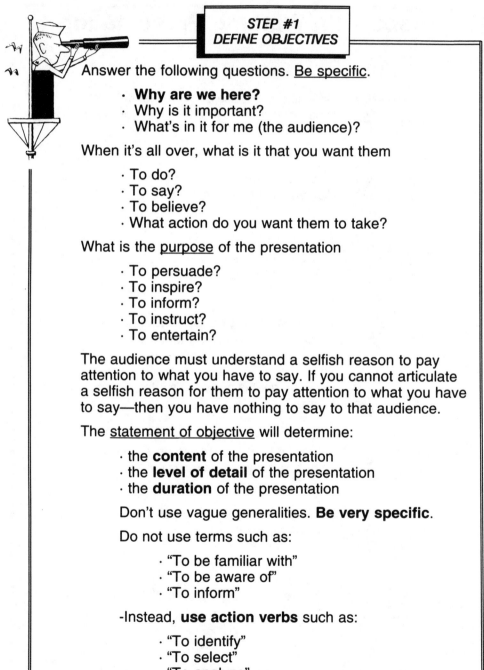

STEP #1
DEFINE OBJECTIVES

Answer the following questions. <u>Be specific</u>.

- **Why are we here?**
- Why is it important?
- What's in it for me (the audience)?

When it's all over, what is it that you want them

- To do?
- To say?
- To believe?
- What action do you want them to take?

What is the <u>purpose</u> of the presentation

- To persuade?
- To inspire?
- To inform?
- To instruct?
- To entertain?

The audience must understand a selfish reason to pay attention to what you have to say. If you cannot articulate a selfish reason for them to pay attention to what you have to say—then you have nothing to say to that audience.

The <u>statement of objective</u> will determine:

- the **content** of the presentation
- the **level of detail** of the presentation
- the **duration** of the presentation

Don't use vague generalities. **Be very specific**.

Do not use terms such as:

- "To be familiar with"
- "To be aware of"
- "To inform"

-Instead, **use action verbs** such as:

- "To identify"
- "To select"
- "To analyze"

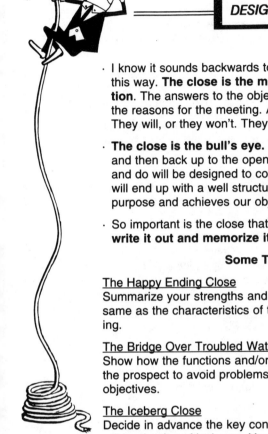

· I know it sounds backwards to design the close first, but look at it this way. **The close is the most important part of the presentation**. The answers to the objectives as embodied in the close are the reasons for the meeting. At the close we either did, or didn't. They will, or they won't. They are sold, or they aren't.

· **The close is the bull's eye.** So, if we focus on the bull's eye first, and then back up to the opening and the body, everything we say and do will be designed to contribute to and enhance the close. We will end up with a well structured presentation that has singleness of purpose and achieves our objective.

· So important is the close that we should do what the Pros do— **write it out and memorize it.**

Some Types of Closes

The Happy Ending Close
Summarize your strengths and advantages, and show them to be the same as the characteristics of the ideal "X" described in your opening.

The Bridge Over Troubled Waters Close
Show how the functions and/or features of your product/service allow the prospect to avoid problems, minimize risk, and achieve their objectives.

The Iceberg Close
Decide in advance the key conclusions of your presentation. These will be the tips of icebergs. Your close (with an iceberg visual) will then summarize the facts, proof, examples and references that are below the water that support the tip of each iceberg.

The Final Exam Close
Prepare a visual with a one-sentence summary of each of the major points. Leave a key word in each sentence blank. This serves as a review, a summary, and reinforces important points.

The Jigsaw Puzzle Close
Break the customer's objective into multiple parts. Then show how your recommendation solves each part—providing a total solution.

The Emotional Close
Dale Carnegie said, "When dealing with people remember you are not dealing with creatures of logic but with creatures of emotion." So close with an emotional quote from a respected authority.

STEP #3
CREATE OPENING

· **The opening is the second most important part of the presentation.**

· You are an unknown quantity for only 120 seconds. **Your most listened-to sentence is your first.** Your preparation (or lack of it), your attitude, and your style become apparent almost instantly.

· The good news is—we have already designed the close. So our **opening can be constructed as a "set-up" for the close**.

Here are some **ideas for capturing interest and keeping attention** in the first two minutes:

- · Ask a provocative question.
- · Use a famous quote that relates to your subject.
- · State a startling fact or statistic.
- · Appeal to human interest by telling a story or personal experience that relates to your subject.
- · Refer to a recent news item or incident that relates to your subject.
- · Be sure you answer these questions:

> Why are we here?
> What is the agenda?
> What are your credentials?
> What's in it for them?

Here's what not to do:

- · Don't tell jokes unless you are naturally humorous.
- · Don't give dictionary definitions of words.
- · Don't say "I'm happy to be here" unless your body language gives the same message.
- · Don't apologize.
- · Don't show an organization chart and tell the history of your department or your organization.
- · Don't turn the lights out.
- · Don't just read every word on every visual and nothing else.
- · And above all, **please don't read a script**.

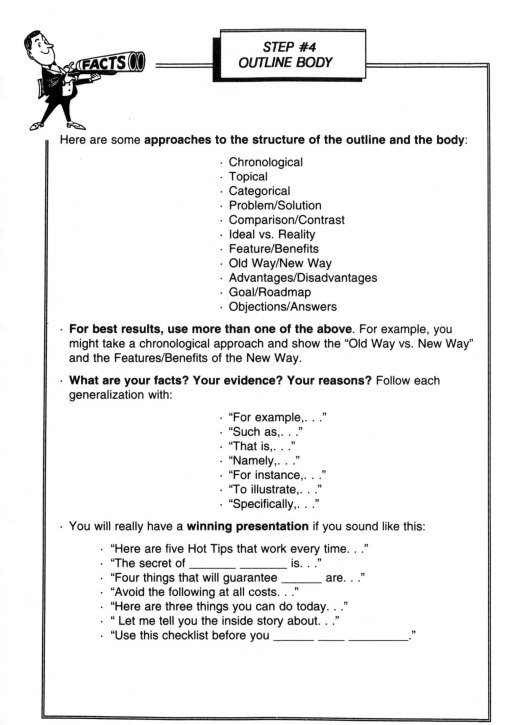

STEP #4
OUTLINE BODY

Here are some **approaches to the structure of the outline and the body**:

- Chronological
- Topical
- Categorical
- Problem/Solution
- Comparison/Contrast
- Ideal vs. Reality
- Feature/Benefits
- Old Way/New Way
- Advantages/Disadvantages
- Goal/Roadmap
- Objections/Answers

- **For best results, use more than one of the above**. For example, you might take a chronological approach and show the "Old Way vs. New Way" and the Features/Benefits of the New Way.

- **What are your facts? Your evidence? Your reasons?** Follow each generalization with:

  - "For example,. . ."
  - "Such as,. . ."
  - "That is,. . ."
  - "Namely,. . ."
  - "For instance,. . ."
  - "To illustrate,. . ."
  - "Specifically,. . ."

- You will really have a **winning presentation** if you sound like this:

  - "Here are five Hot Tips that work every time. . ."
  - "The secret of _____ _____ is. . ."
  - "Four things that will guarantee _____ are. . ."
  - "Avoid the following at all costs. . ."
  - "Here are three things you can do today. . ."
  - " Let me tell you the inside story about. . ."
  - "Use this checklist before you _____ ____ _____."

STEP #5
ADD SPICE

Our next mission is to breathe life, fun, excitement and human interest into our presentation by adding spice. You can be dull, dry, and boring or you can be alive, exciting and interesting. Just add a touch of "hot spice" every six to eight minutes. People will remember the spice. And if you relate the spice to a key point, people will remember the key point. If you don't, they won't, because people forget 75% or more of what they hear in 24 hours or less.

Examples of Hot Spice

- Startling visual aids
- The proper use of humor
- Human interest stories
- Planned questions
- Analogies
- War stories
- Testimonials
- Demonstrations
- Even gimmicks <u>if</u> they relate to the subject

- Hot Spice is particularly effective if it has to do with one of these subjects:

- Sex	- Fame
- Money	- Glory
- Opportunity	- Popular
- Trouble	- Profit
- Weight	- Love
- Health	- Fear

- Your brilliant insights, sound arguments, and startling revelations will fall on deaf ears if the minds of the audience are out to the beach. **Good content alone is no assurance of an effective presentation**. And great content never saved a bad delivery.

- The solution? A touch of Hot Spice every six to eight minutes—otherwise known as **industrial showmanship**.

STEP #6
VISUAL AIDS

Why use visual aids?

· People are 43% more likely to be persuaded.
· People will pay 26% more money for the same product or service.
· You can tell the same story in 25-40% less time.

If a picture is worth a thousand words, then one picture is worth eight minutes of talking. Good visual aids stimulate interest, clarify, substantiate, and reinforce what has been said.

Q: What does a good visual aid look like?
A: It looks like a billboard on an interstate highway that people can read going by at 65 MPH.

Here are the **rules of the road for good visual aids**. The first three are the most important:

· Simplify.
· Simplify.
· Simplify.
· Use color—the world's worst visual is a black and white of a typewritten page.
· Translate numbers into pie charts, bar charts, or graphs.
· Minimize words. Don't use complete sentences. Use bullets only.
· Use pictures, graphs, symbols, and cartoons that relate to the subject.
· Only one key point per visual.
· The best visual is the real thing—next best is a picture of it.
· Select the visual aid media that you are comfortable with and have confidence in.
· Keep the lights as bright as possible. You are the message. The greatest visual of all is <u>YOU</u>.

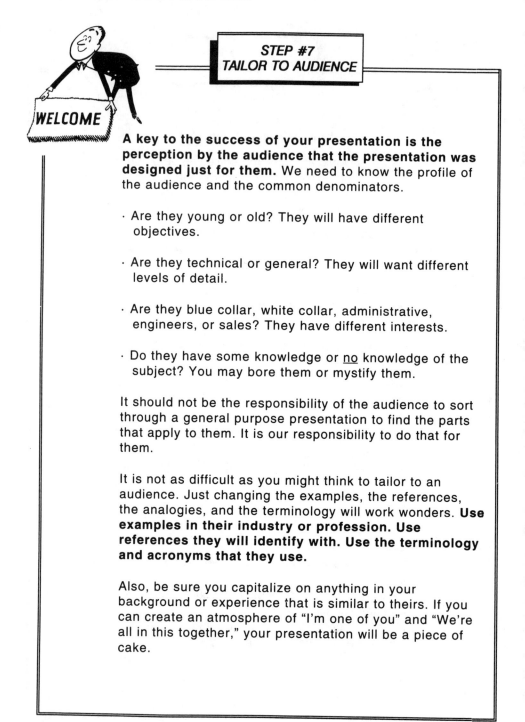

STEP #7
TAILOR TO AUDIENCE

A key to the success of your presentation is the perception by the audience that the presentation was designed just for them. We need to know the profile of the audience and the common denominators.

· Are they young or old? They will have different objectives.

· Are they technical or general? They will want different levels of detail.

· Are they blue collar, white collar, administrative, engineers, or sales? They have different interests.

· Do they have some knowledge or <u>no</u> knowledge of the subject? You may bore them or mystify them.

It should not be the responsibility of the audience to sort through a general purpose presentation to find the parts that apply to them. It is our responsibility to do that for them.

It is not as difficult as you might think to tailor to an audience. Just changing the examples, the references, the analogies, and the terminology will work wonders. **Use examples in their industry or profession. Use references they will identify with. Use the terminology and acronyms that they use.**

Also, be sure you capitalize on anything in your background or experience that is similar to theirs. If you can create an atmosphere of "I'm one of you" and "We're all in this together," your presentation will be a piece of cake.

**STEP #8
CREATE
CHEAT SHEETS**

The ultimate fear of all presenters is not that they will stumble and fumble through a presentation, but that they will suddenly go blank.

That will never happen if you use "cheat sheets." **A cheat sheet has the first three to five words, or the key words, you will say for every major point.** It also has questions to ask and sketches of graphics you would draw. It is a shorthand script of the presentation. It tells you what to say, what to do, and when to do it.

Cheat sheets can be:

- Around the sides of frames on transparencies
- A page underneath each transparency
- Lightly written on flip charts
- A page per slide or per multiple slides

Often no cheat sheet is necessary since the content of many of your visuals will be their own cheat sheet.

With cheat sheets you don't have to memorize. If you memorize:

- It sounds like it's memorized.
- It's difficult to sound warm and sincere.
- You may, indeed, forget and go blank.

With cheat sheets you don't have to read. If you read:

- It sounds like you're reading.
- It will lack sincerity and conviction.
- You will have little or no eye contact with your audience, and 55% of the impact of your presentation is non-verbal communications.

With a cheat sheet you make the dream of all presenters a reality:

- You have the power of key words and phrases.
- The surrounding words flow automatically and smoothly.
- You convey the appearance of giving an exciting presentation extemporaneously.

**STEP #9
REHEARSE**

There are three compelling reasons for you to rehearse:

1. **It is the single best solution to the problem of tight nerves and sweaty palms.** You have good reason to be nervous and sweaty if you don't know what you're going to say or how you're going to say it. The concept of "I'll play it by ear" is a guarantee of mediocrity at best.

2. **The second reason is even more important than the first— 95% of how well your presentation is going to go is determined before you even start.** That means <u>rehearse</u>. There is no fast-food line to giving a good presentation. You have to pay your dues. Do not do what the pros would never try—perform without practice.

3. **If you don't rehearse, your audience will know you haven't.** That says to your audience, "I don't think you're very important. If you were, I would be better prepared." Remember, in the mind of your audience the quality of your presentation is a mirror image of the quality of your product, your service, your support, and your people.

The right way to rehearse is to duplicate the conditions of your presentation. That means:

- Rehearsing in the actual room (if possible)
- Using the actual visual aids
- Going through the actual movements and gestures
- Saying the actual words

There is no substitute for doing the real thing the real way.

You Will Win the Trophy

· If you have a passion for the subject.

· If you know 75% of everything there is to know on the subject. (That's not hard to do. If you read the three best books on any subject, you will be in the top 5% of the people in the world in your knowledge of that subject.)

· If for every major point you:

> Tell a story
> Have a quote
> Give an example
> Use appropriate humor

· If you remember the three things an audience will not forgive:

> Not being prepared
> Not being committed
> Not being interesting

Getting Good, Getting Better—The Critique

All the great speakers were bad speakers at first.
Ralph Waldo Emerson

Is the applause at the end a recognition of a good presentation, or a celebration that it's finally over?

If you have followed the Presentation Planning Guide then you cannot fail. But you can get better. However good you are today, you can be three times better tomorrow. We get better by doing two things:

- Rehearsing and doing
- Fixing the flaws

We have covered the subject of rehearsing, so let's focus on fixing the flaws.

Like the game of golf, practice will make you better—up to a point. If, however, there is a fundamental flaw in what you are doing, no amount of practice will correct it. To correct it, the flaw must first be identified, and then corrective action taken.

In presenting as in golf, you will probably be the last to know what your flaws are. The good news is that once you find out what your weaknesses are, they are easier to correct than your golf game.

You can identify and correct the problems in your presentation by the use of technology, or the use of human beings. For best results, we recommend both.

The most powerful tool for identifying flaws is the videotape. It is also good for correcting the obvious. The impact of seeing yourself do the same stupid thing over and over is like being hit with a cold bucket of water. You will grit your teeth and swear that you will never do that again. In the world of presenting there is nothing that will give you religion as fast as seeing yourself sinning on camera. It's interesting that the video camera is also used to identify the sins of the golf swing.

If you don't have access to video, you can at least borrow a cassette recorder and tape the audio portion of your presentation. This will allow you to easily identify problems in the area of pitch, pace, volume, pauses, and so forth.

The video and cassette tape also give you a record of questions asked by the audience. You need to carefully think through the questions. Consistent questions are a clue that your explanation is incomplete or confusing. They may also indicate areas of interest to the audience that had not occurred to you.

The videotape and audio cassette are strong medicine for correcting the obvious. But video is not enough. Like the golfer trying to improve, you need professional help. Get it from an independent, unbiased, but critical observer whose judgment you respect, and who will give you candid comments.

The best observer or critic is someone who is experienced in giving presentations themselves. It might be an associate, a colleague, a member of a professional group, or someone who is on the program with you. If nothing else, pick a friend whose judgment you respect. In fact, it will be helpful if you can arrange for multiple people to critique your presentation.

What you want them to do is *not* give you the big picture, where we ask them at the end of our presentation the question, "Well, what did you think of it?" What you want is a detailed evaluation of the components of your presentation. To accomplish this, we need to place in the hands of our critics a detailed checklist of items to evaluate.

Remember that we are looking for flaws: very specific areas that need improvement. While the critics are at it, we would like to also know our major strengths. This will keep us out of a deep depression when we review our flaws. Figures 17A, B, C , and D tell us what to do and how to do it in each major area of our presentation. These are summarized on one page in Figure 17E. And Figure 17F is a critique form to record our performance.

Brace yourself. This may hurt. Avoid the temptation to become defensive and start explaining the reasons why you do or don't do certain things. The audience doesn't know or care why you do or don't. The simple rule of this game is: The audience is right.

The problem is that we judge ourselves by our intentions, but others judge us by our performance. And Daniel Webster said, "The world is governed more by appearance than by reality." And so it is that our audience will measure us as shown in Figure 17G.

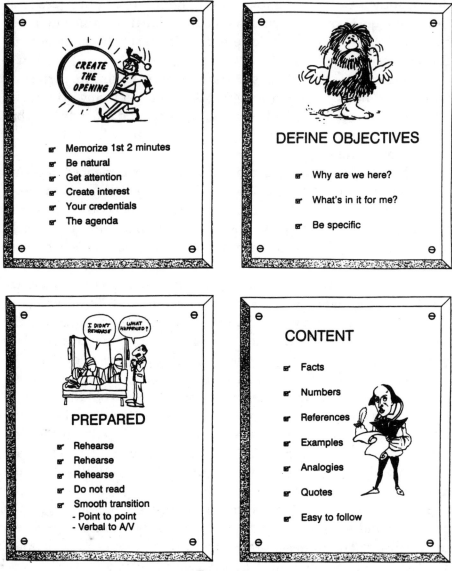

Figure 17A

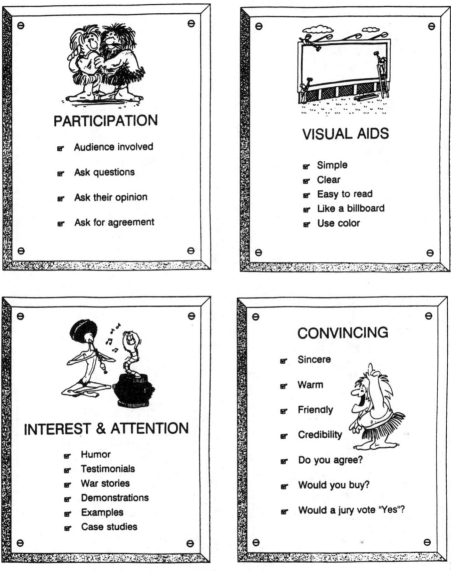

Figure 17B

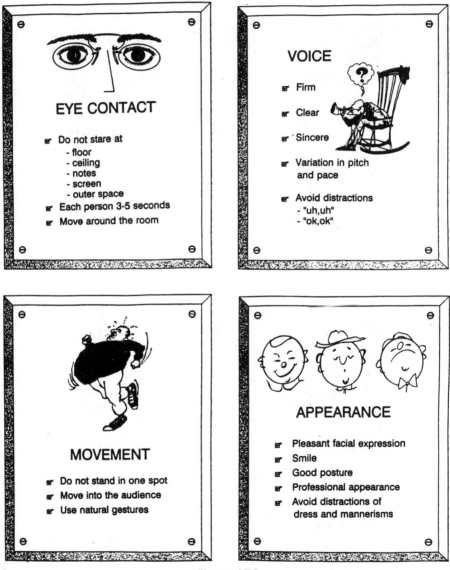

Figure 17C

Figure 17D

GETTING GOOD, GETTING BETTER

Opening   Memorize the first two minutes. Get attention and interest, and create a good first impression. What are your credentials? What is the agenda?

Objective   Why are we here? When it's all over, what is it that you want them to do, to believe, or what action do you want them to take? Answer the question, "What's in it for them?"

Prepared   Rehearse, Rehearse, Rehearse. Do not read. Notes should be key words and phrases only.

Content   Use good facts, numbers, references, examples, analogies, quotes, etc. Make sure you have good organization—very logical—easy to follow—flows well.

Participation   Get the audience involved. Plan in advance to ask questions, ask for agreement, ask their opinion. Refer their company, their department, to their job. Use their terminology acronyms.

Visual Aids   Visuals should be simple, easy to read and understand—like a billboard. Use pictures, drawings, graphs, bar charts, pie charts. Use overlays for complex subjects. Use color. Use revelation technique. Visuals should clarify, simplify and emphasize.

Interest   Get interest and keep attention. Use questions, demonstrations, testimonials, war stories, humor (if natural), visual aids, analogies, exercises, case studies, examples, etc.

Convincing   Do you agree? Would you buy? Would you sign? Be sincere, warm, friendly. Speak with knowledge, conviction, and enthusiasm. Establish credibility. A jury would vote "Yes."

Eye Contact   Do not stare at floor, ceiling, your notes, the screen, or outer space. Have three to five seconds of eye contact with each person—move around the room.

Voice   The voice should be firm, clear, sincere. Vary pitch and pace. Avoid distractions— "uh," "ah," "ok,ok."

Movement   Do not stand in one spot. Move into the audience. Use natural gestures to add emphasis.

Appearance   Keep a pleasant facial expression. Smile. Maintain a comfortable relaxed posture and a professional appearance. Avoid distraction of dress and mannerisms.

Strong Close   Memorize the last two minutes. Summarize. Ask for agreement. Ask for the order. Ask for action.

Figure 17E

GETTING GOOD, GETTING BETTER

	High |_|_|_|_|_|_|_|_|_|_| Low	Comments
Opening	|_|_|_|_|_|_|_|_|_|_|	_____
Objective	|_|_|_|_|_|_|_|_|_|_|_|	_____
Prepared	|_|_|_|_|_|_|_|_|_|_|_|	_____
Content	|_|_|_|_|_|_|_|_|_|_|_|	_____
Participation	|_|_|_|_|_|_|_|_|_|_|_|	_____
Visual Aids	|_|_|_|_|_|_|_|_|_|_|_|	_____
Interest	|_|_|_|_|_|_|_|_|_|_|_|	_____
Convincing	|_|_|_|_|_|_|_|_|_|_|_|	_____
Eye Contact	|_|_|_|_|_|_|_|_|_|_|_|	_____
Voice	|_|_|_|_|_|_|_|_|_|_|_|	_____
Movement	|_|_|_|_|_|_|_|_|_|_|_|	_____
Appearance	|_|_|_|_|_|_|_|_|_|_|_|	_____
Strong Close	|_|_|_|_|_|_|_|_|_|_|	_____

STRONG POINTS	WORK ON	DISTRACTIONS

Figure 17F

Figure 17G How the audience will measure us.

General audience critiques, when used in conjuction with the detailed checklist, will allow you to really zero in and fine tune your presentation.

The difficulty with the audience critiques is that they tend to be too general. If a critique sheet says the presentation was poor and of little value, that doesn't tell you a lot about what to do to correct it.

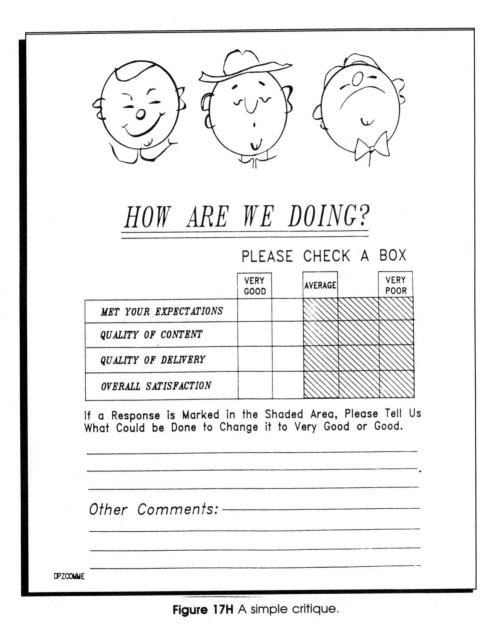

Figure 17H A simple critique.

PRESENTATIONS PLUS WORKSHOP

Course Evaluation

1. What was most useful or meaningful about the Workshop? _____

_____

2. What was least meaningful? _____

3. How do your rate the following? **Please circle.**

	Excellent		Average		Poor
Overall program	5	4	3	2	1
Met your expectations	5	4	3	2	1
Knowledge of Instructor	5	4	3	2	1
Instructor's presentation style	5	4	3	2	1
Usefulness of content/information	5	4	3	2	1
Effectiveness of Workbook	5	4	3	2	1
Effectiveness of visuals	5	4	3	2	1
Relevance to your job	5	4	3	2	1

4. Was the material: ____Too advanced   ____Too basic   ____Just right

5. Was the pace: ____Too fast   ____Too slow   ____Just right

6. Was class involvement: ____Too much   ____Too little   ____Just right

7. On a scale from 1-5 (5 being high), how do you rate your ability to use the skills learned? ____

8. On a scale from 1-5, how do you rate your commitment to use the skills learned?____

9. Please make any additional comments or suggestions about the Workshop. (Continue on back) _____

_____

_____

_____

Figure 17I A better critique.

```
        MARKETING EDUCATION                      COURSE NUMBER _____
        FINAL COURSE EVALUATION                  CLASS  NUMBER _____


Name: _____
If you would like a response to your comments, please add:
PROFS NODE/ID: _____     Phone # _____

Please rate the following about the Marketing Education Course you just attended.
                                                    Very                    Very
OVERALL COURSE SATISFACTION                         Good Good Avg. Poor Poor
    1.  Overall course satisfaction........................  1    2    3    4    5

COURSE CONTENT & DELIVERY
    2.  How the course met objectives......................  1    2    3    4    5
    3.  Depth of course content............................  1    2    3    4    5
        If 3, 4, or 5, please circle Too Deep or Too Shallow
    4.  Length of course...................................  1    2    3    4    5
        If 3, 4, or 5, please circle Too Long or Too Short
    5.  Quality of course materials........................  1    2    3    4    5
    6.  Value of exercises.................................  1    2    3    4    5
    7.  Ability of instructors.............................  1    2    3    4    5
    8.  Effectiveness of delivery approach.................  1    2    3    4    5

APPLICATION TO YOUR JOB
    9.  Relevance of course content to your job............  1    2    3    4    5
   10.  Ability now to apply course skills.................  1    2    3    4    5
   11.  Opportunity now to apply course skills.............  1    2    3    4    5
   12.  Availability of course when needed.................  1    2    3    4    5

OTHER
   13.  Enrollment process.................................  1    2    3    4    5
   14.  Education facilities...............................  1    2    3    4    5


Please give us your comments, especially if any response is marked average, poor, or very
poor. (Use back of form if necessary) _____
_____
_____
_____

What would you add or delete from the course? _____
_____
_____

What other education requirements do you have? _____
_____
_____


Please select your job function. (Circle one of the following)
    Trainee:                          Rep   SE    Other_____
    Marketing Representative:         GT    GA    AF    NA    Other_____
    Systems Engineer:                 5H    5G    5D    5F    Other_____
    Manager:              Marketing  Systems  Engineering  Branch  Other_____
    Business Partner
    Other. Explain_____

How long have you been in your current area of responsibility? (Circle one)
    0-1 YR    1-3 YRS    3-5 YRS    5+ YRS
```

Figure 17J A comprehensive critique.

CRITIQUE

E = Excellent   S = Satisfactory   N = Needs Improvement

CATEGORY	RATING	REMARKS
Objective	E, S (N)	Not sure what objective was
Structure & Flow	E, S (N)	No planned structure
Preparedness	E, S (N)	No signs of advanced preparation
Participation	E, S (N)	Over-use of questions
Bad Habits	E, S (N)	Interrogates person asking questions
Visual Aids	E, S (N)	No visual aids
Confidence	E, S (N)	Not sure of himself, always asking questions
Time Control	E, S (N)	Never finishes at a scheduled time
Control	E, S (N)	Too flexible, loses control
Close	E, S (N)	Lets audience come to its own conclusions
Use of English	E, S (N)	Speaks in heavy Greek accent
Appearance	E, S (N)	Dresses in old sheet
Personality	E, S (N)	Prone to suicide by poison

Figure 17K If your critiques aren't good—take heart. This fellow's weren't, either. His name was Socrates.

But it doesn't have to be that way. Critiques can be designed to give you a lot of information about your presentation, its value, and about the audience. Figures 17H, I, and J show three critiques from simple to comprehensive.

All this criticizing will result in a list of a few areas that need improvement. What we must do now is prioritize the list. It is not possible to work on all areas at the same time. So pick the big one that stands out the most and work on it first. Then you can move on to the other areas.

Audience critiques can be a humbling experience. Remember we said that out of every 100 people there's at least one nut. They will sure show themselves on the critiques. You won't meet everyone's expectations. Some will be bored—a few may be hostile. So don't be surprised and don't take it personally. Even the President of the United States gets some bad reviews.

There was a fellow a long time ago who got terrible critiques. An example of one of his critiques is Figure 17K. They were so bad that it's hard to believe that he was so good. But he was. In fact, he is known today as one of the greatest teachers in all of recorded history. Maybe you've heard of him.

The Road to Glory

All of us travel many roads. Some are crooked, some are bumpy, some lead us to a dead-end. But occasionally, either by plan or by accident, we find a smooth road that leads straight ahead to personal glory. Perhaps some of you are on such a road today. If you are, then the contents of this book can make your journey faster, smoother—and the glory greater.

If you have not yet found your road to glory, this may be your horse to ride. There is a critical shortage of good presenters. Whatever your profession or occupation, opportunity is knocking and inviting you into the spotlight.

There are immediate openings at the top of the mountain. Furthermore, you do not have to be brilliant, talented, a workaholic, or have advanced degrees to get there.

The world is full of brilliant people who are poor. Consider, for example, the 55,000 members of MENSA (I.Q. of 135 required to get in the back door). Their average annual earnings are less than a plumber.

As for talent—nothing is more common than unsuccessful people with talent. Most of history's greatest achievements have been accomplished not by the most talented, but by people of average skill who had other more important characteristics.

Is hard work the answer? Hardly. There are millions of people who have worked hard all their lives, yet today they are living on Social Security.

Do education and advanced degrees make a difference? Yes, but—there is nothing so common as a well-educated person. The world is full of educated derelicts. And did you know that 15% of all millionaires did not finish high school?

May I summarize for you 20 years of study by Dr. Charles Garfield as documented in 318 pages of his book "Peak Performers." He concludes that peak performers are:

- Not born — they are made
- Not superhuman with special talents—but average people like you and me
- Not workaholics—but they are committed to results, not activities.

And so indeed there are extraordinary possibilities in ordinary people. As Satchel Paige of baseball fame put it, "Nobody can help being born common, but ain't nobody got to remain ordinary." And so today I invite you to catch the tide—it's at its flood. Answer the knock—it's at your door. It may not pass this way again. The Road to Glory starts today.

Throughout recorded history, man has been looking for common denominators among leaders, winners, and achievers. They are not easy to find, but there is one that is common to all great men and women in history. They all have a mental image—a vivid picture—of themselves in the future having already achieved their goal. They have a dream in the head.

They have an intense commitment to what they do and what they want. High achievers call it by different names—a passion, a mission, a purpose, a deep feeling, or a fire in the belly. They credit their success more clearly to that passion than to aptitude. More to desire than to knowledge or education.

Oliver Wendell Holmes was talking about them when he said, "Every calling is great when greatly pursued."

Man's need for meaning and purpose in life is one of the great drives in human nature. We are built to solve problems, conquer obstacles, and achieve goals. Those who have none wander in circles. They find life aimless and boring and are plagued with depression. They are missing the spark of life.

One of the miracles of the mind is its ability to rationalize almost anything. Unsuccessful people, without exception, have reasons to explain their lack of achievement. Repeated often enough, they come to believe and feel comfortable with their excuses. In time, their excuses become a self-fulfilling prophecy.

Opposed to the fiction of luck is the law of cause and effect, which says that for every effect in our lives there is a specific cause. Since we have the ability to change the causes, we can change the effects. If we wish our lives to be different in the future, we have to change the causes in the present. Life doesn't care who succeeds and who fails—it's up to you. Success is not a pie with only so many slices to go around. The law of cause and effect will prevail. So-called "luck" is what happens when preparation meets opportunity. Success comes not from being dealt a good hand, but in playing well the cards you have. Most of history's greatest achievements were not made by people who were dealt a royal flush, but by those with a pair of jacks.

We can, we should, and we must accept the responsibility for our own destiny. Our future lies not in the stars but within ourselves, to paraphrase Shakespeare. The man upstairs is not our navigator. He gave each of us the intellect and the wherewithal to chart our own course—to write our own book. We have a choice. We alone can use the talent we have.

Only a very few are willing to invest the time and effort to excel. For most the vision is blurred. They cannot see the road ahead. But if you have read this far, then you have a sense of personal destiny.

Good communicators can touch and change the lives of people. They can redirect the future of companies. You can be one of them. You have nothing to lose. You can only be better for the experience. So come along with me. Let's walk this road together. And I believe, *I believe*— I BELIEVE you will walk the road to glory.

INDEX

Wharton School of Business
(University of
Pennsylvania) study and, 4-
5, 6
See also specific visual aids
Visual, reading verbatim with, 22,
88
Visual vs. auditory information,
78-81, 186
Voice, 260, 262
  changing pace of, 94
  characteristics of, 191-192
  problems with, 191
  tone of, 191
  use of, in presentations, 93-94
Voltaire, 21
Volume, 191, 192

W

Wall Street Journal, The, 104
Wall Street Week, 102
Wal-Mart Stores, 104
Walton, Sam, 104
Webster, Daniel, 257
Weight-of-evidence technique, for
  defusing troublemakers, 160
Wharton School of Business

(University of Pennsylvania),
4-5, 6
What can go wrong, in
  presentations, 176-177
"What's in it for me?," 72, 244
Whisperer Troublemaker, The,
  164-165
  how to defuse, 165
Whispering vs. loudness, 94, 233
Who to call for help, 177
Winning presentation
  format of, 247
  steps to, 243-253
Women how to dress, 190
  in management, success factors
    for, 6, 7
  special distractions to avoid, 188
Word combinations, most
  powerful, 118-119
Words avoiding technical, 229
  distracting, 192-193
  enhancing appearance and
    interest of, 229
  minimizing, 249
  misspelled, 100, 129, 194

Y

You Are The Message (Ailes), 113